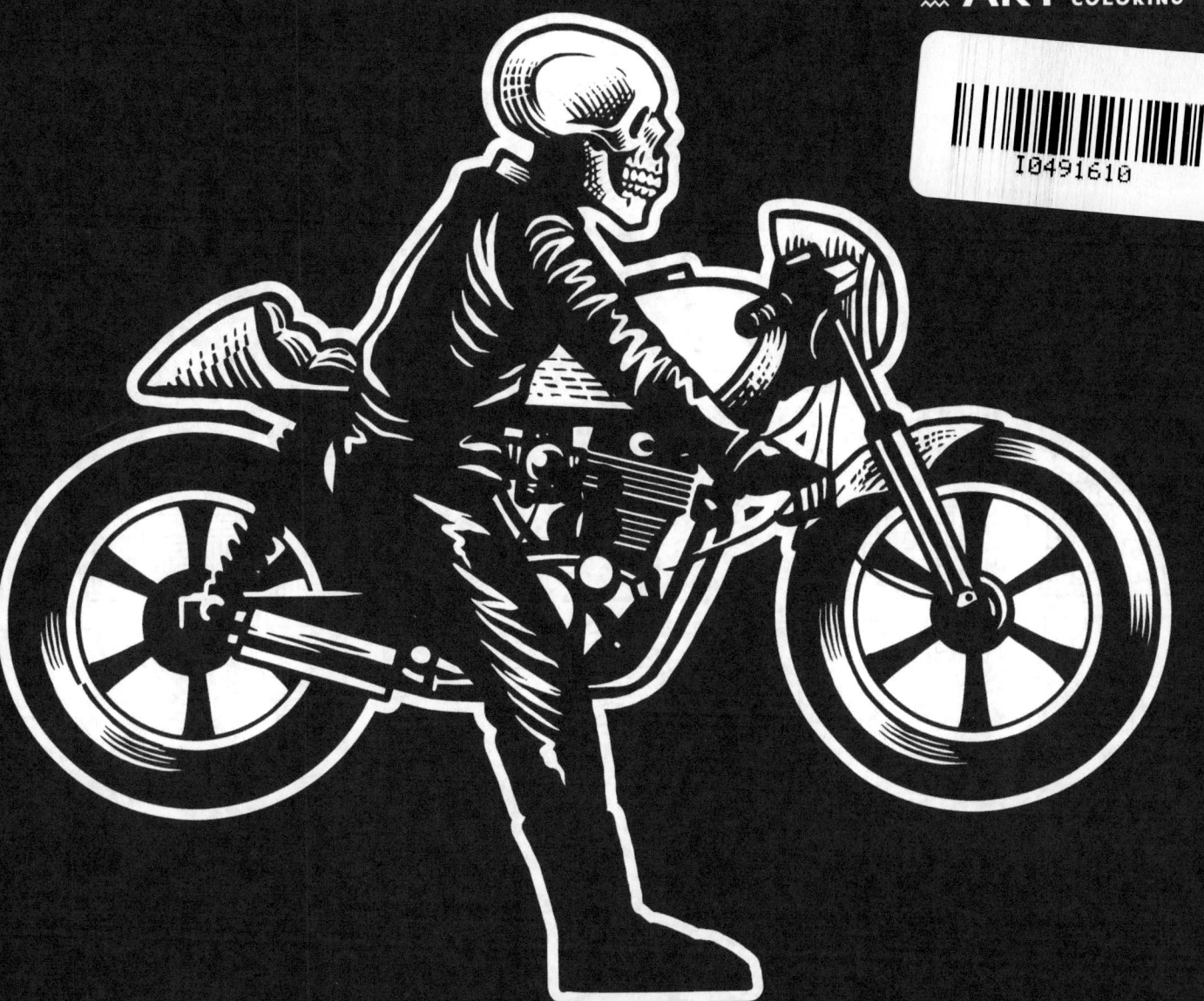

MOTORCYCLE COLORING BOOK FOR TEENS

Black Background

Preview of Coloring Pages

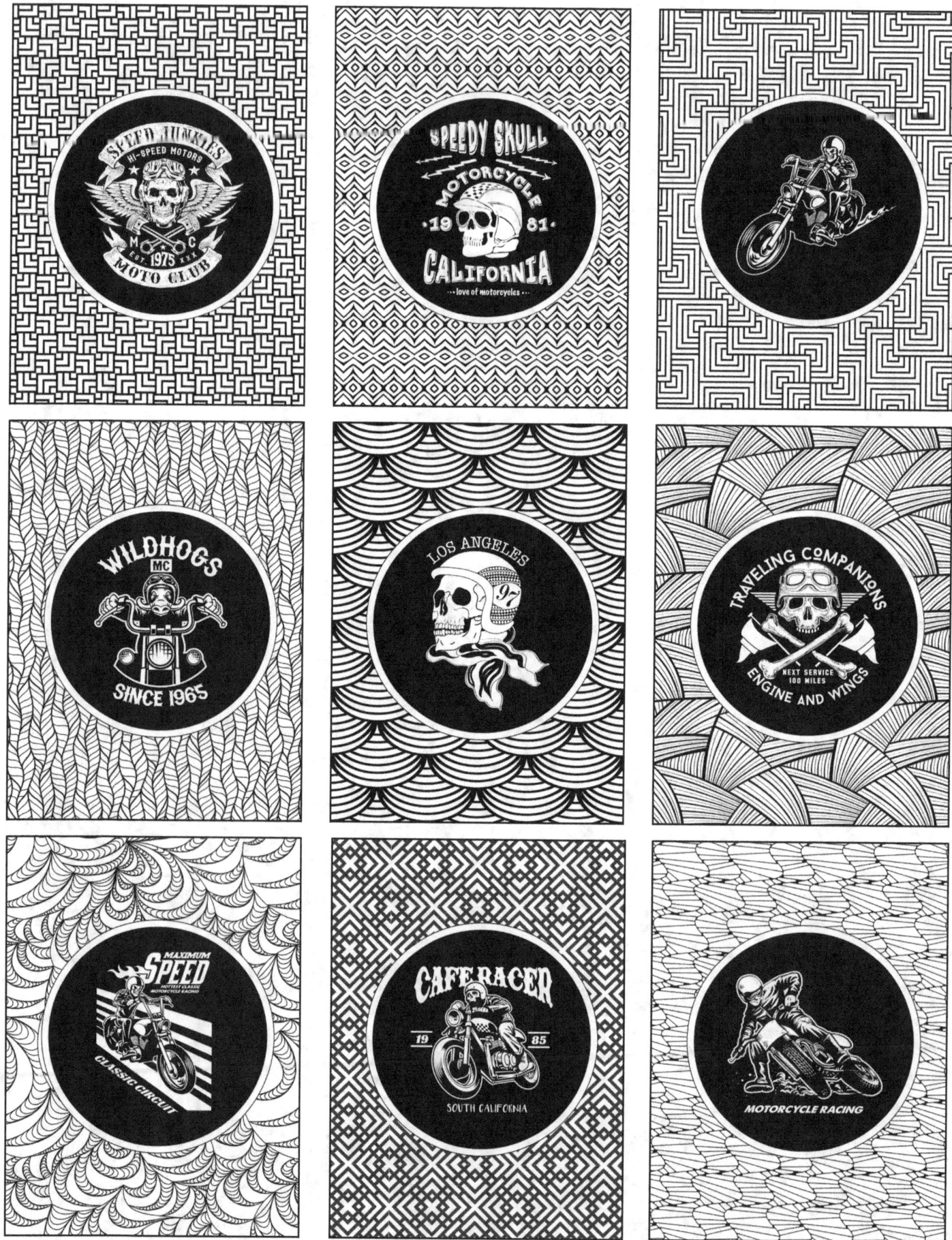

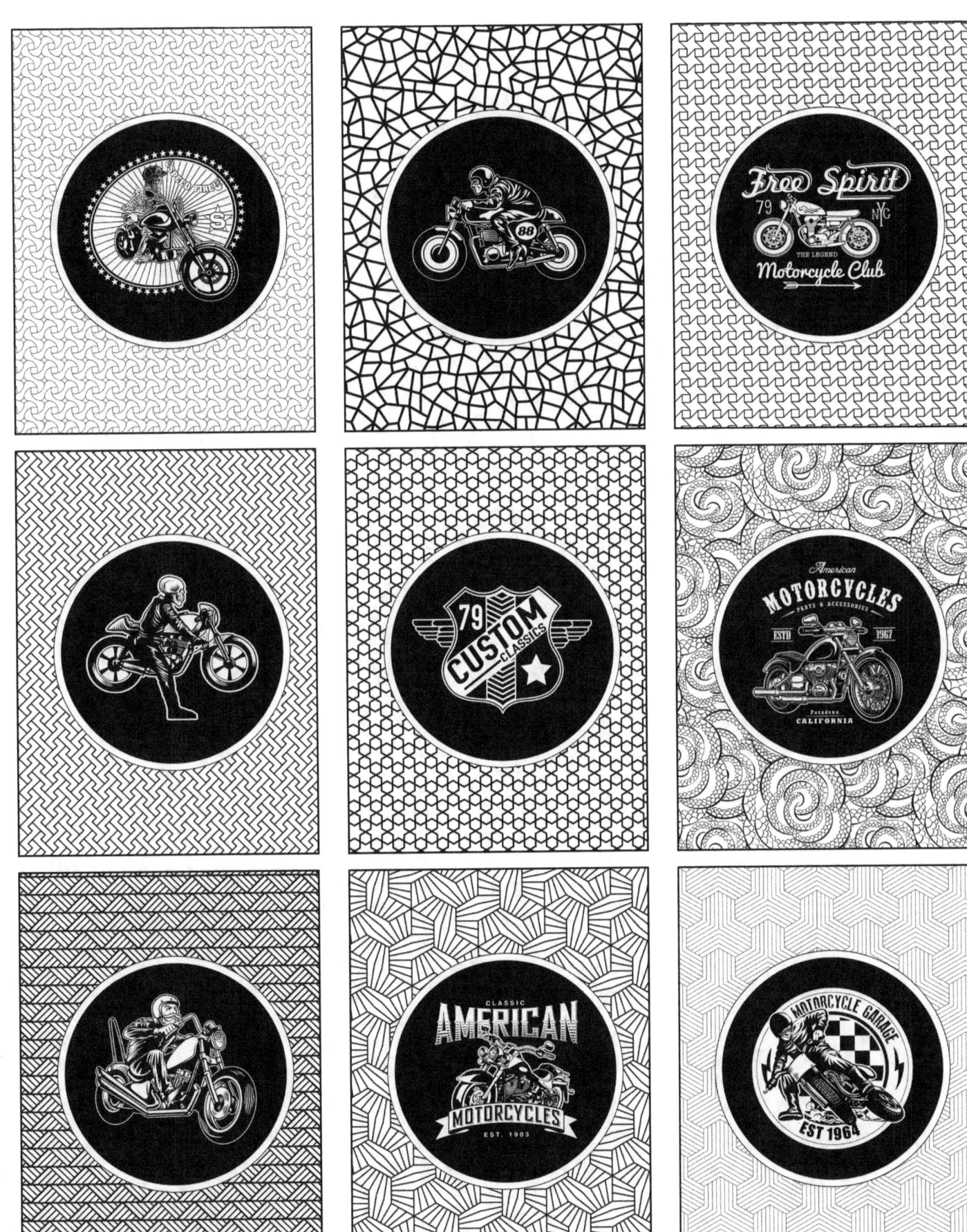

Preview of Coloring Pages

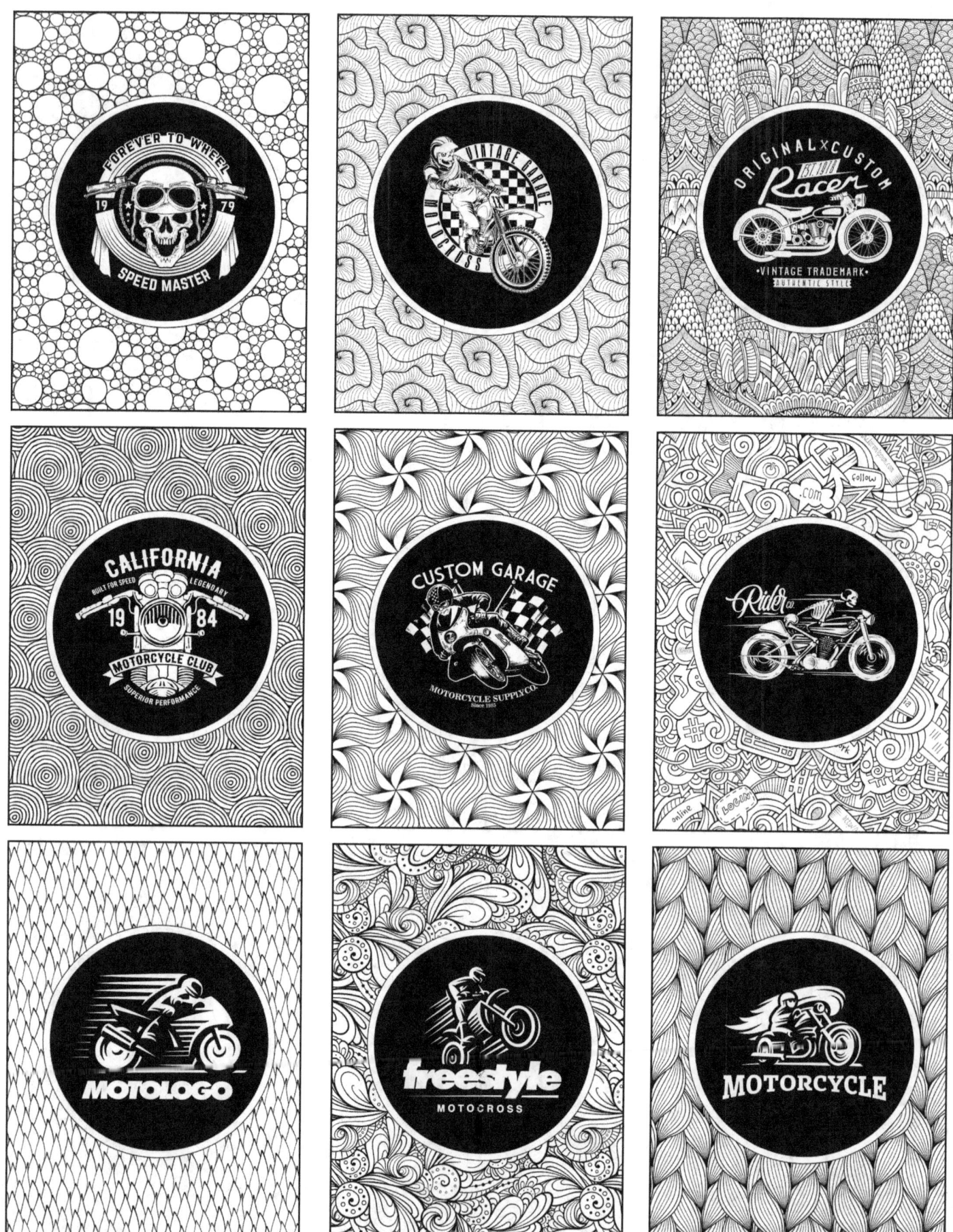

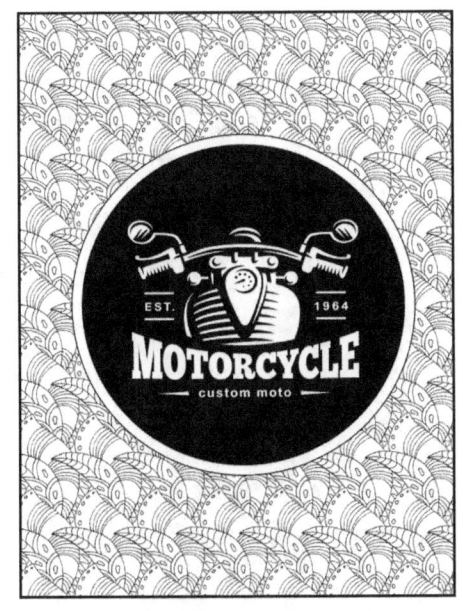
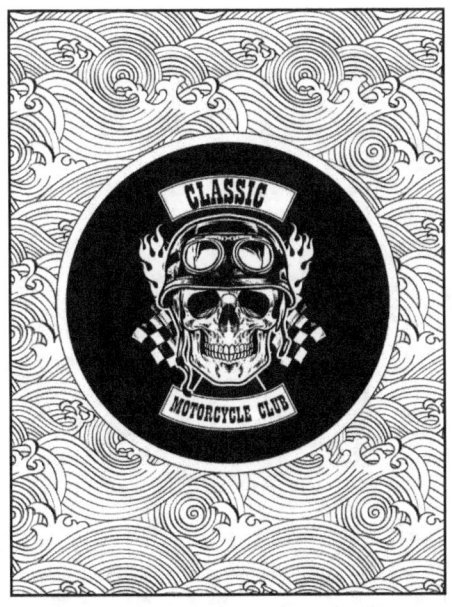
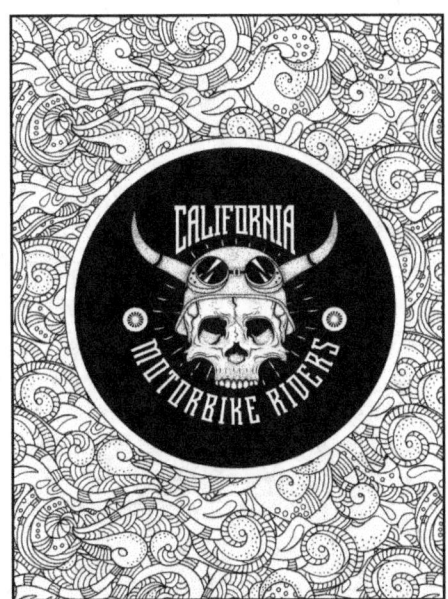

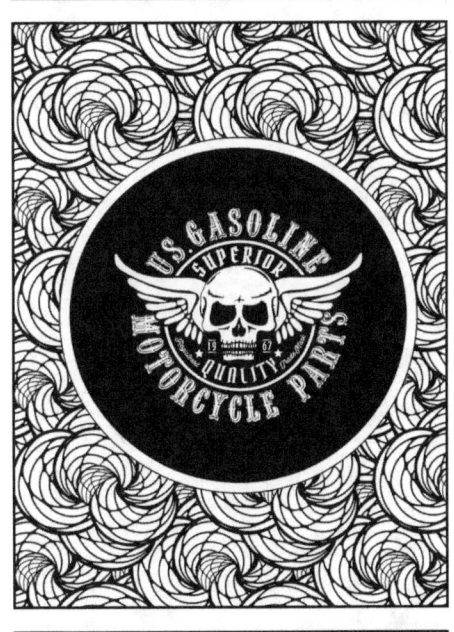
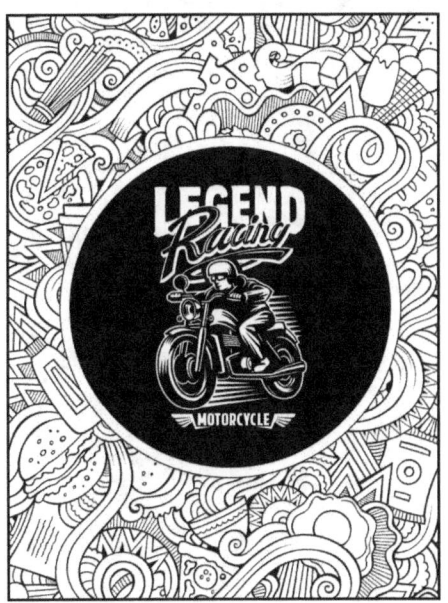
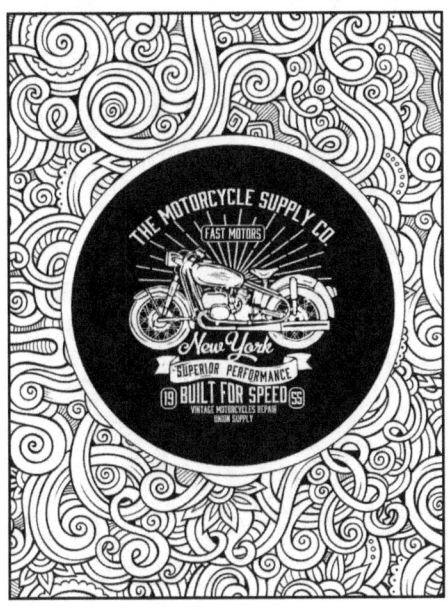
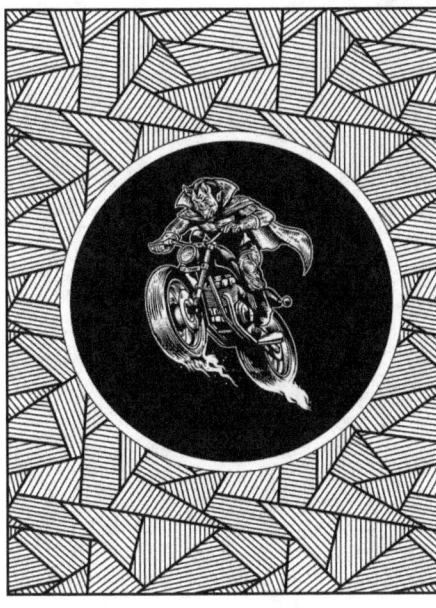

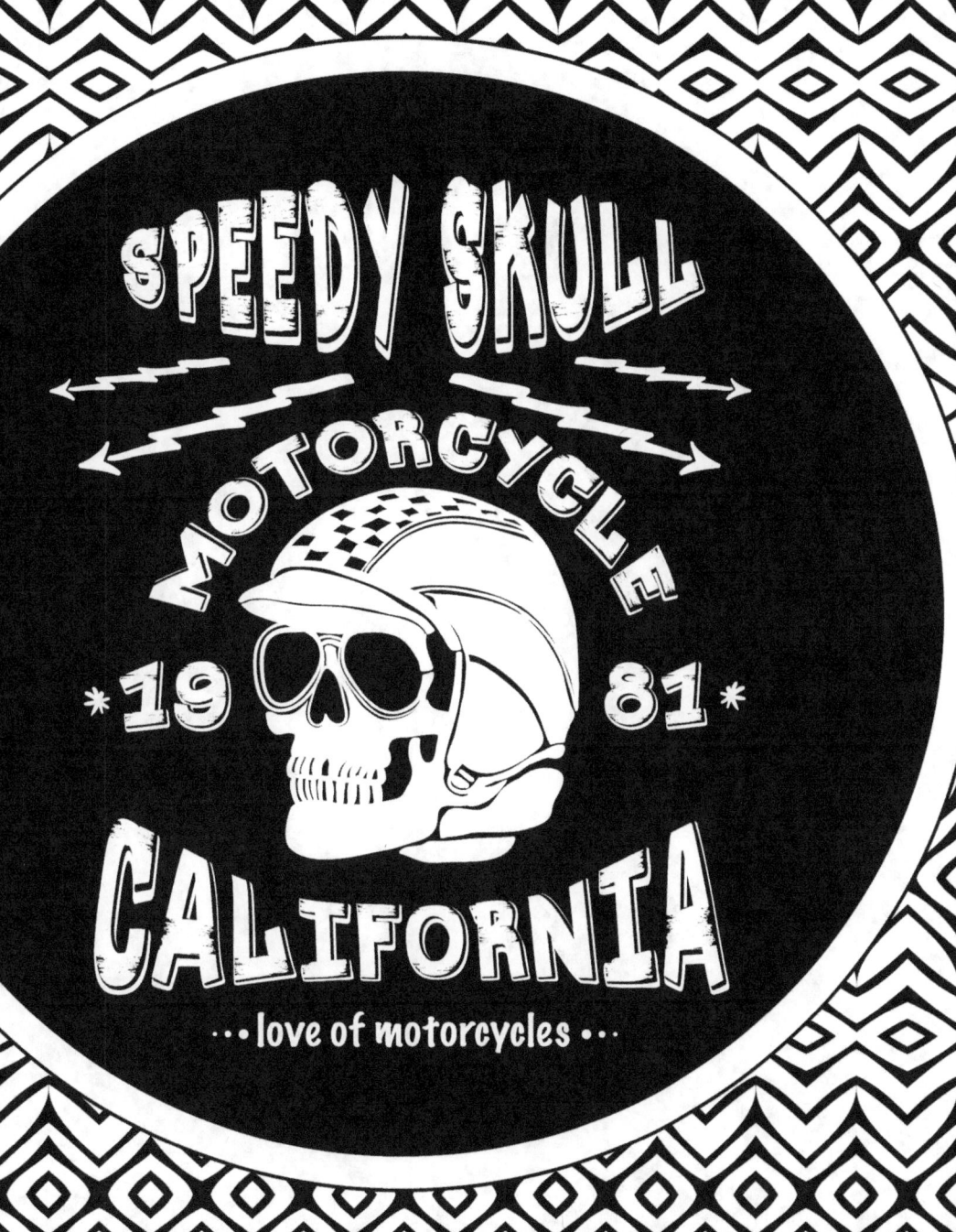

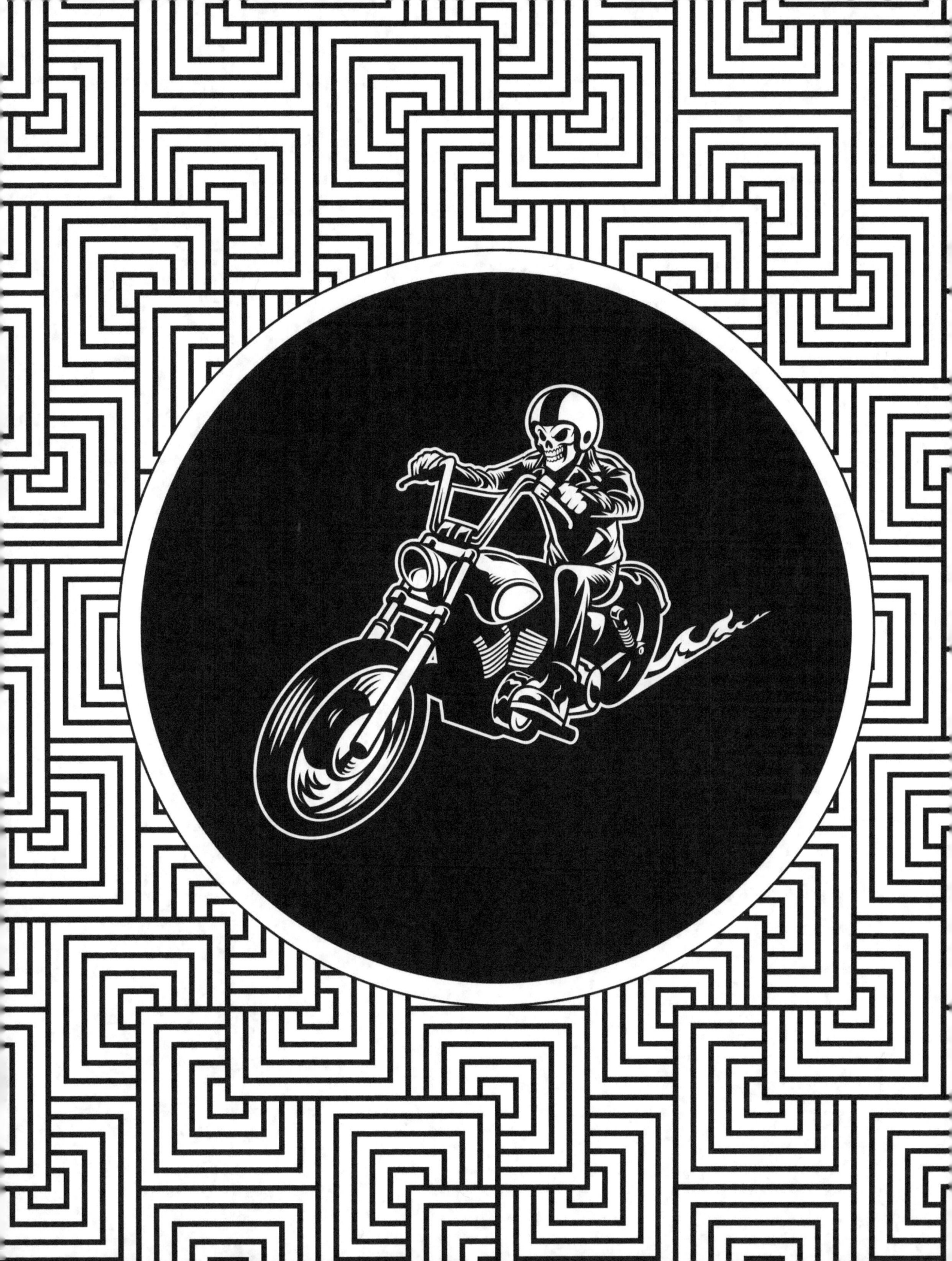

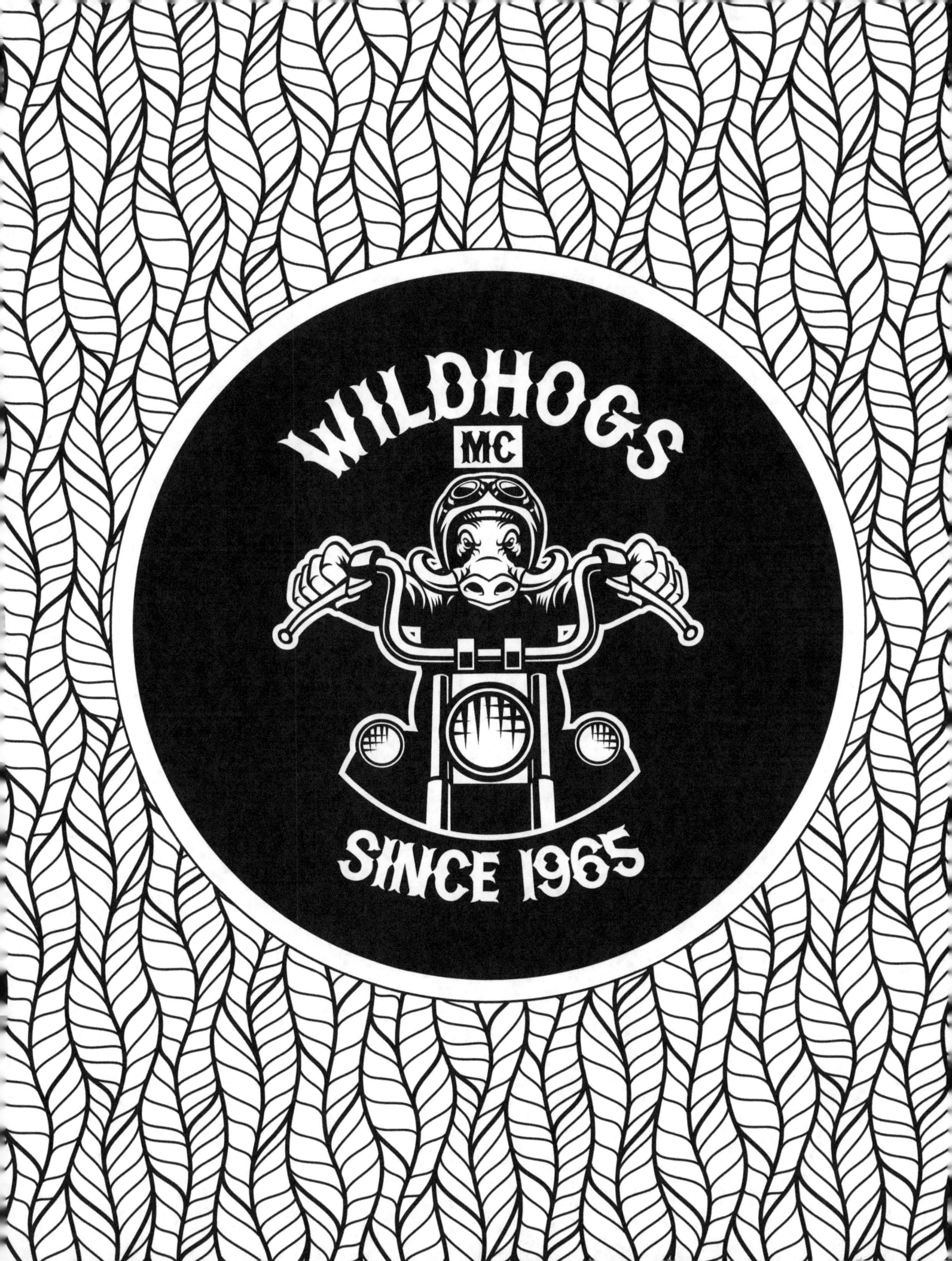

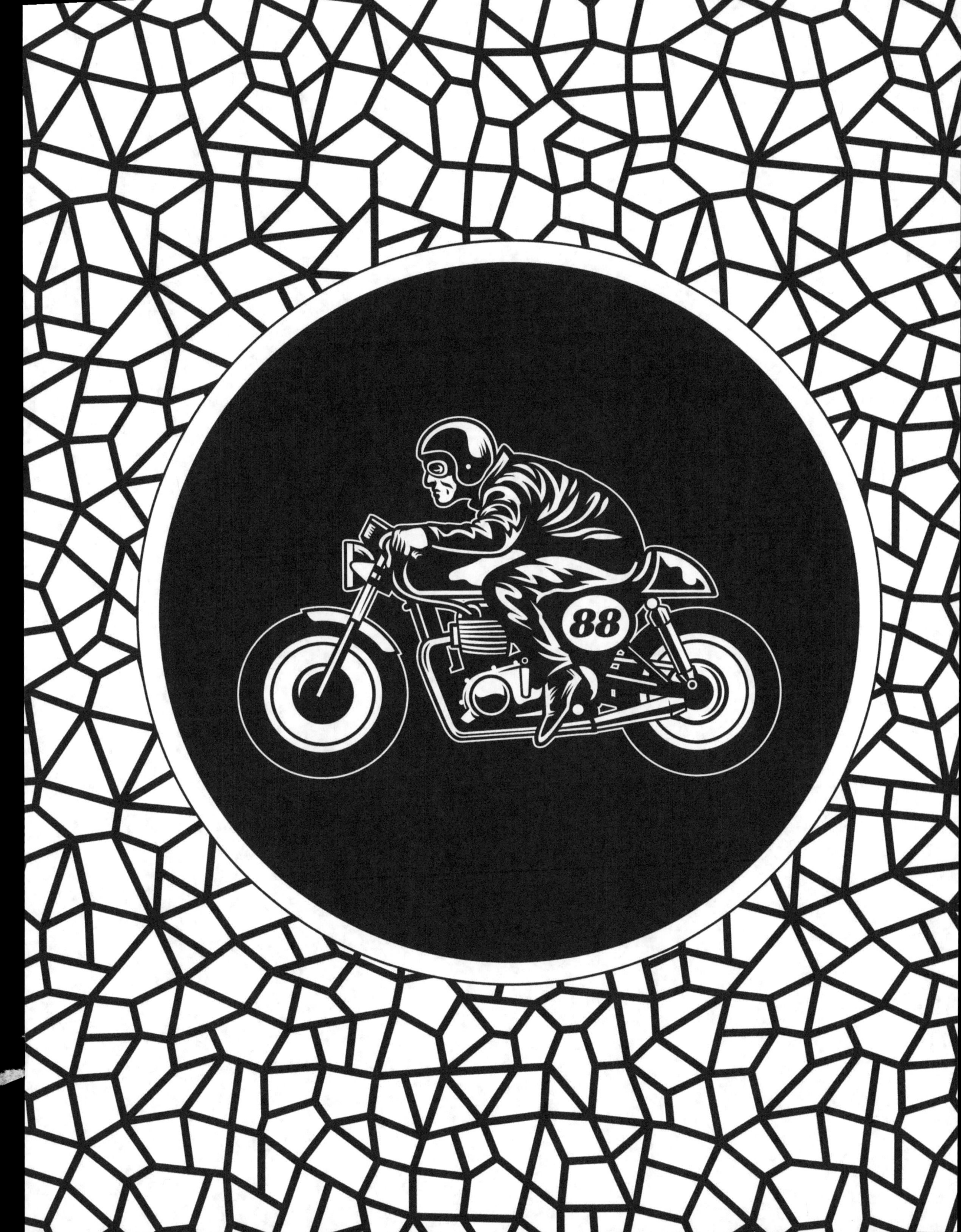

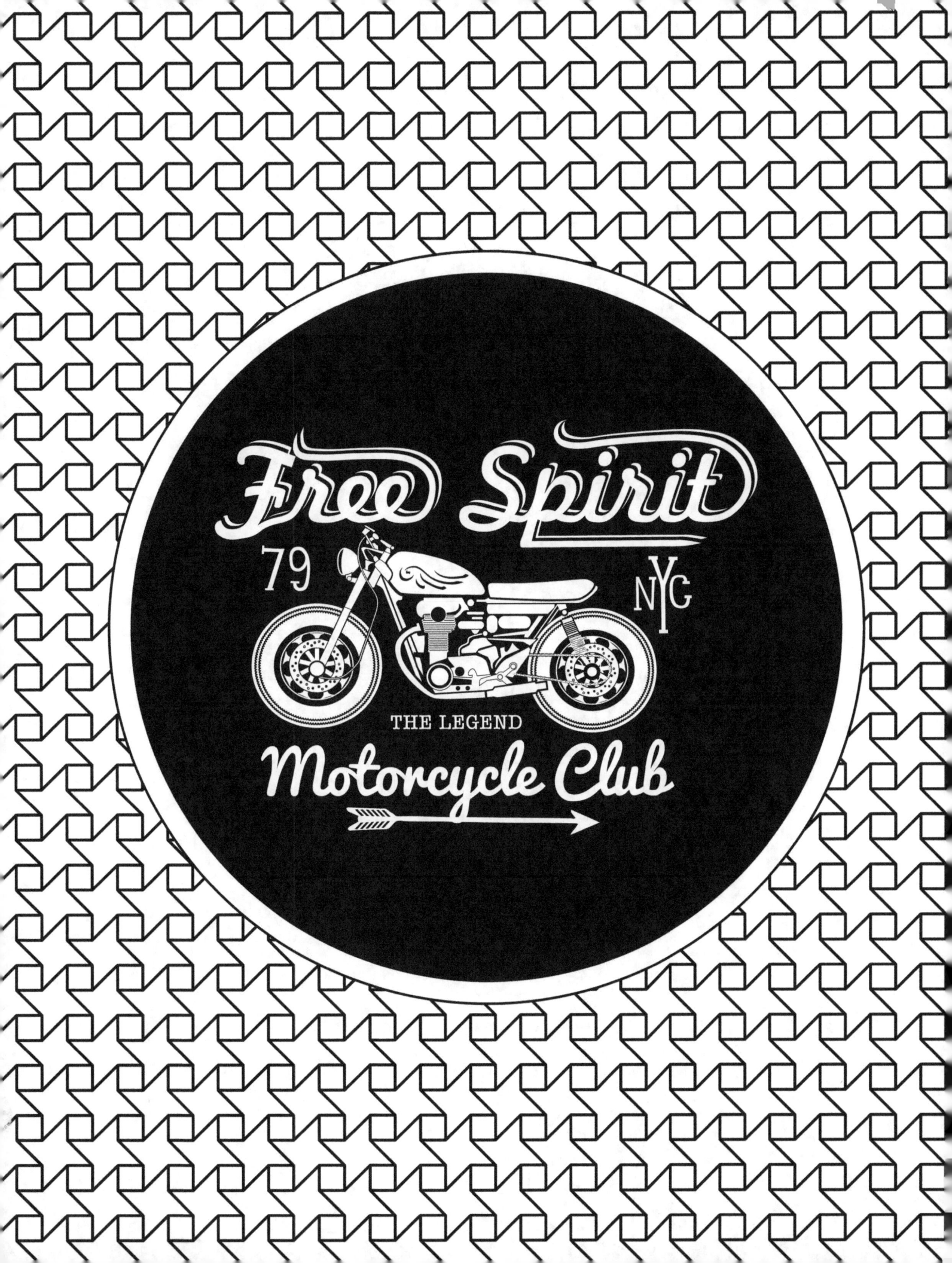

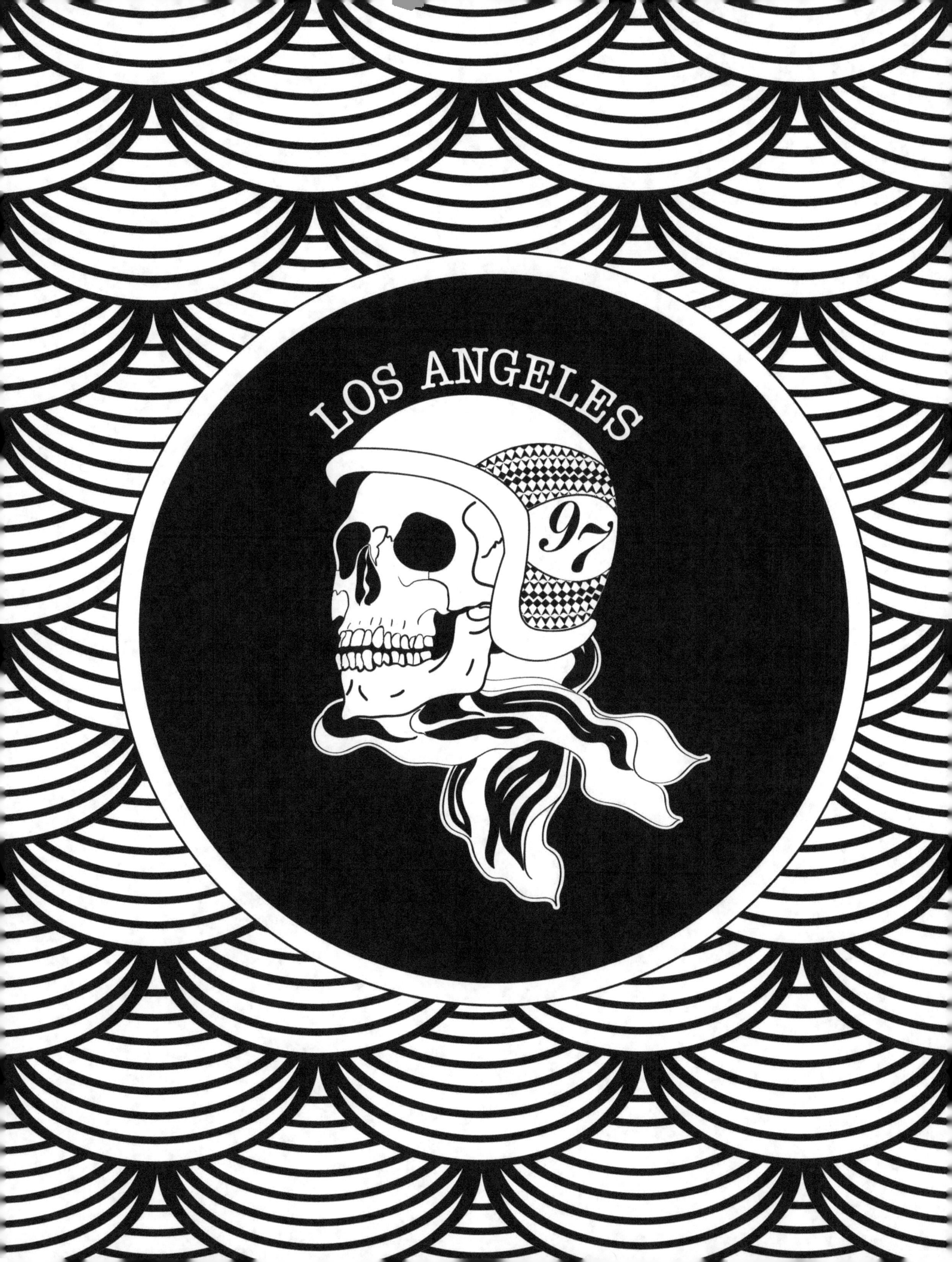

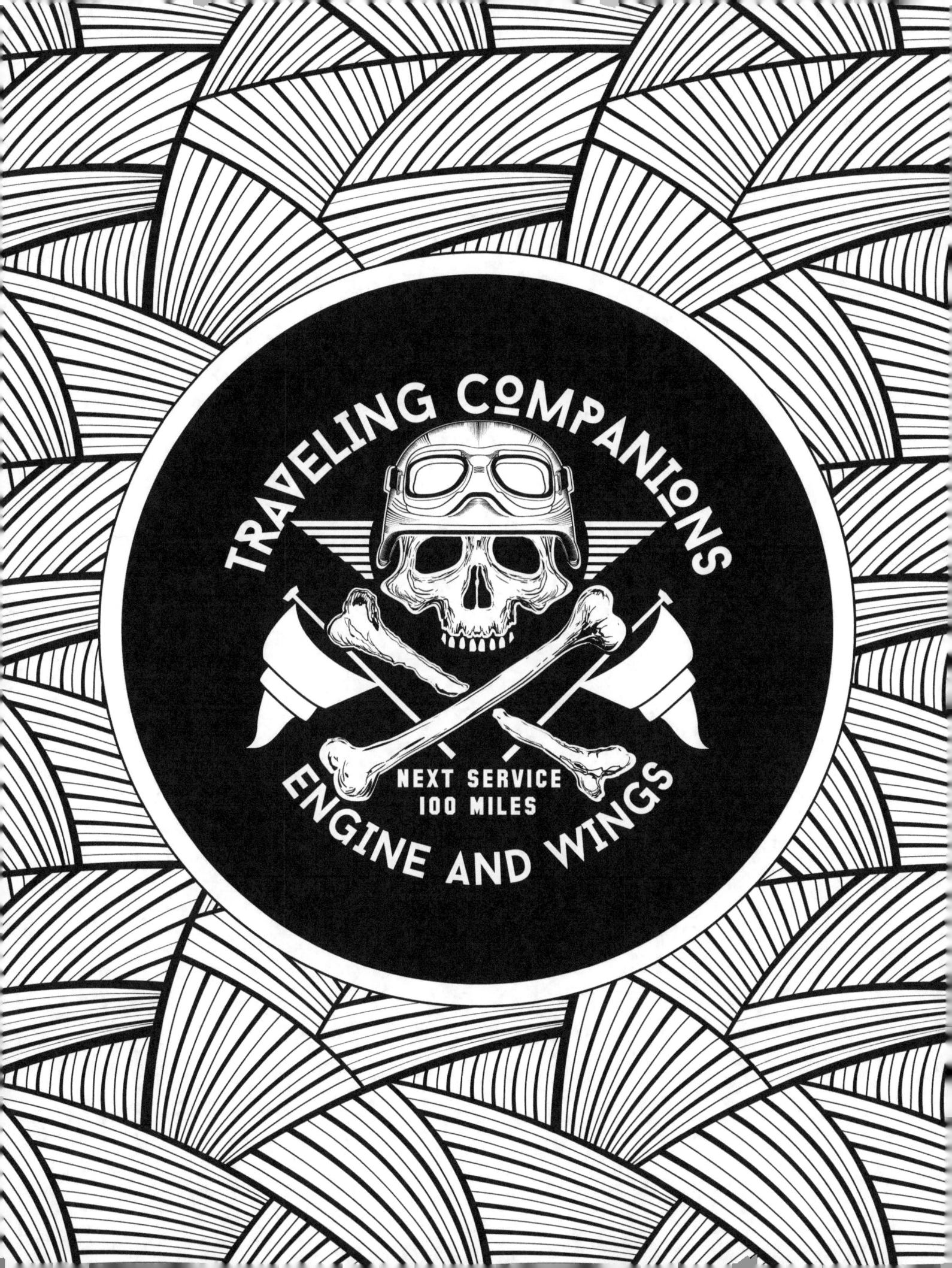

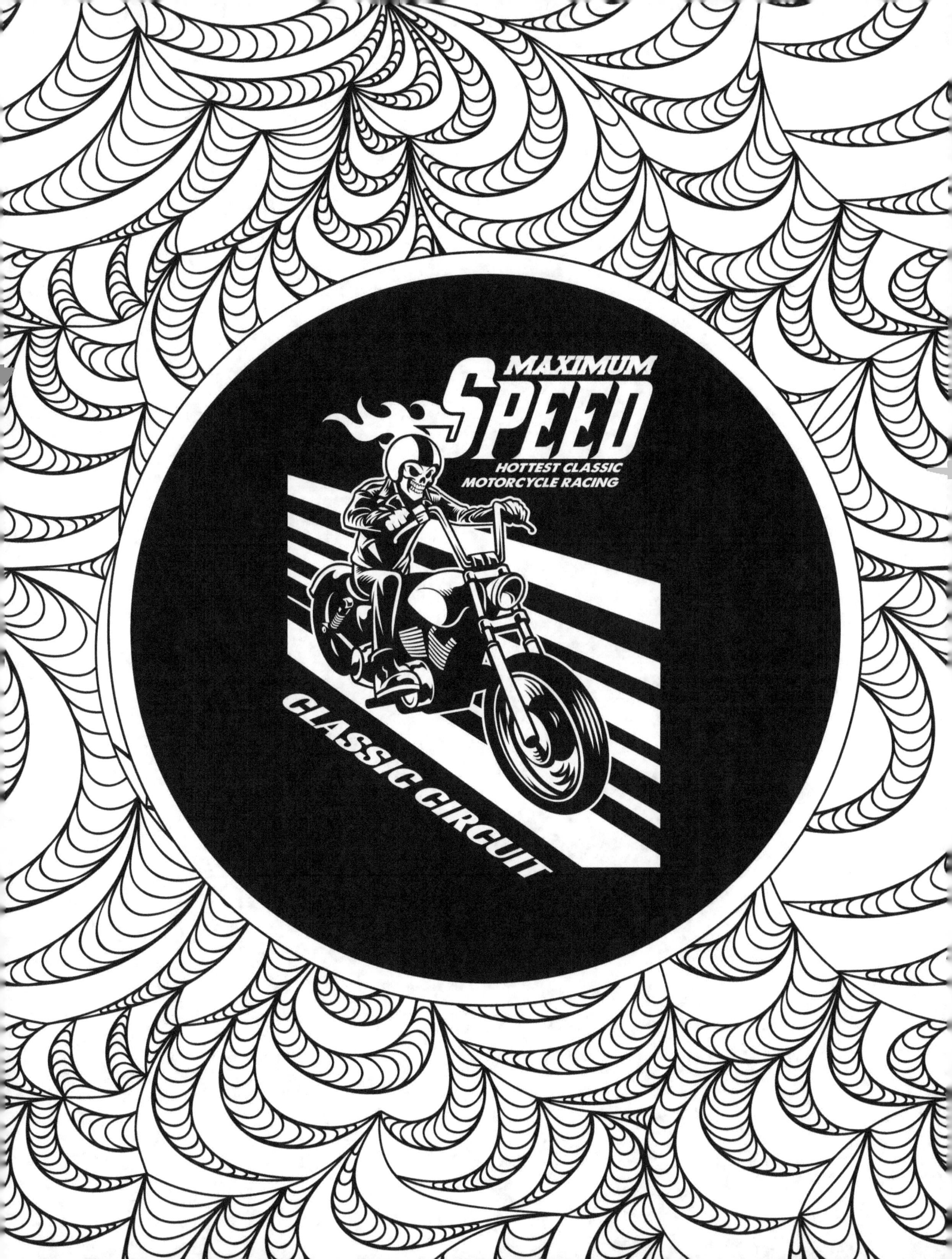

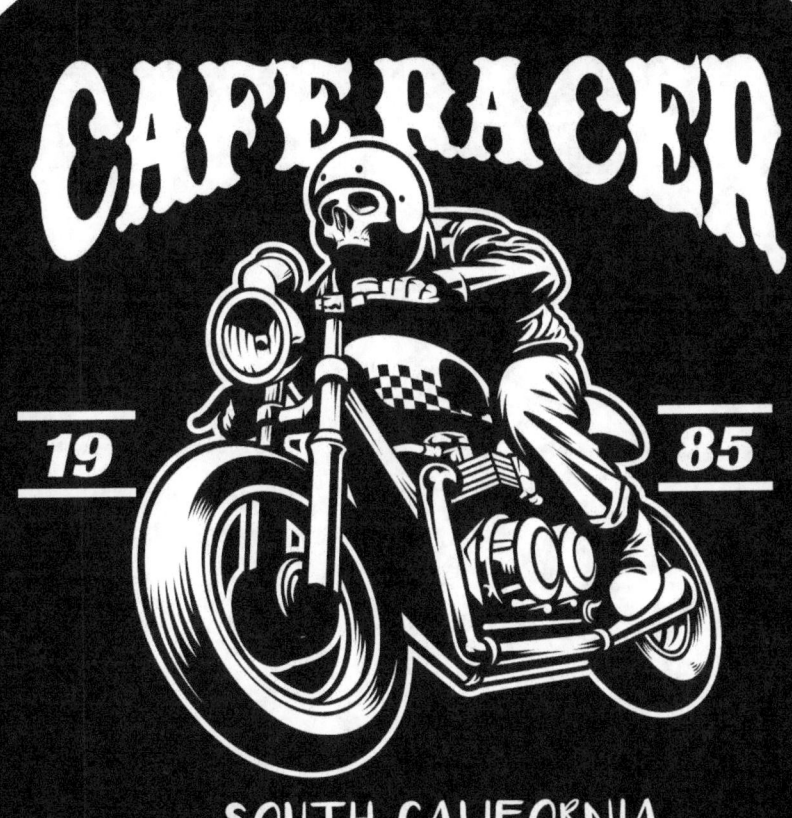

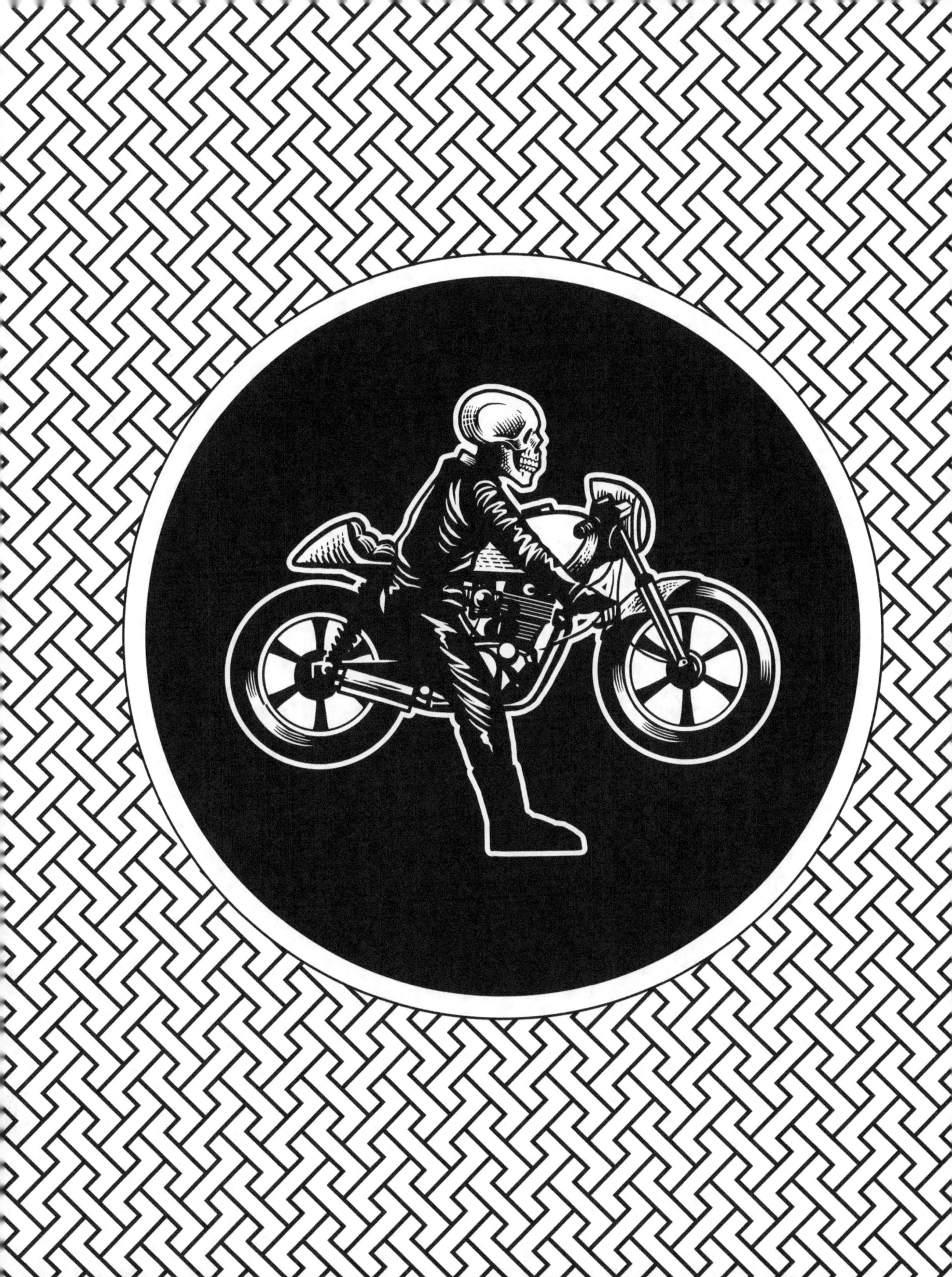

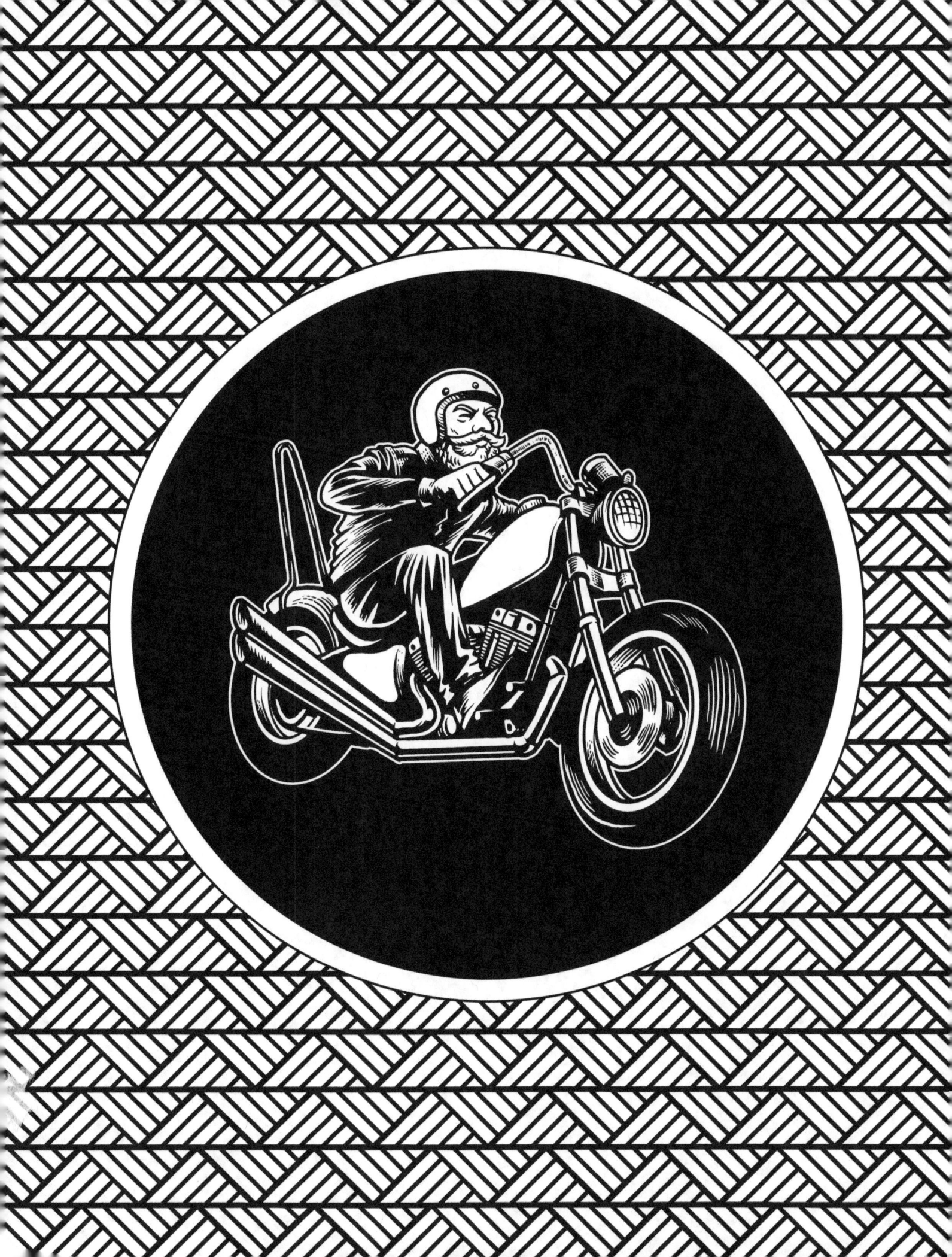

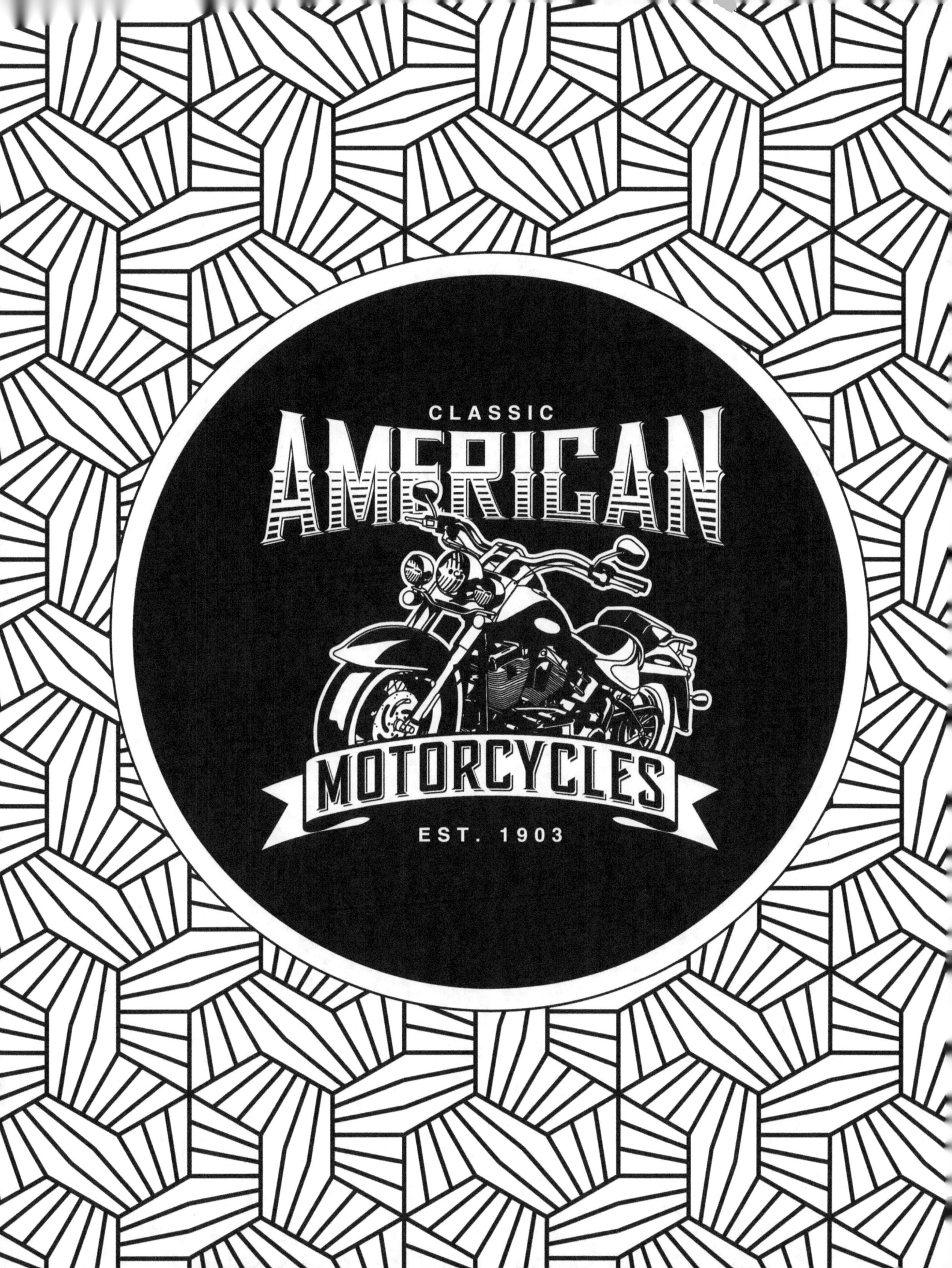

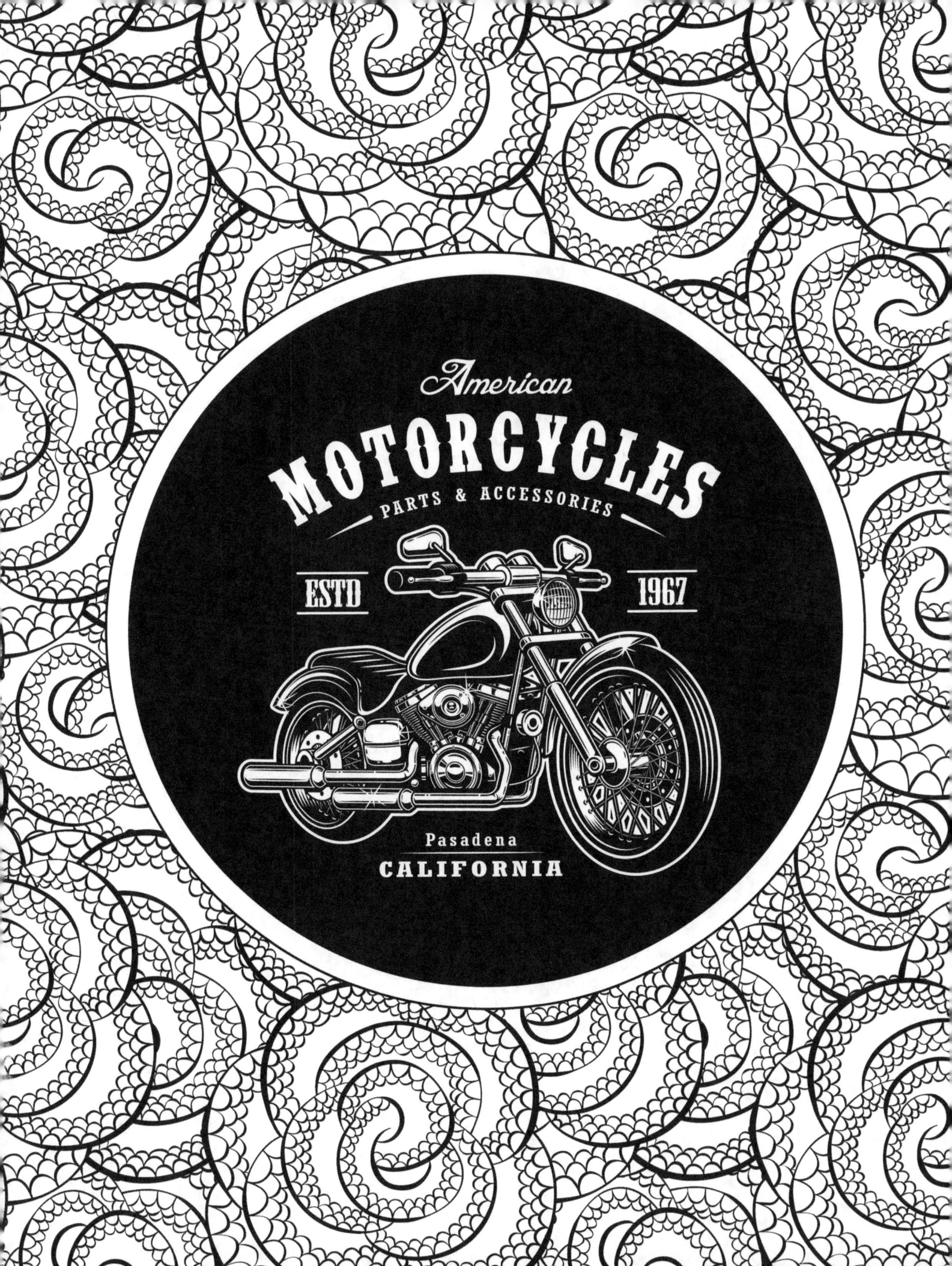

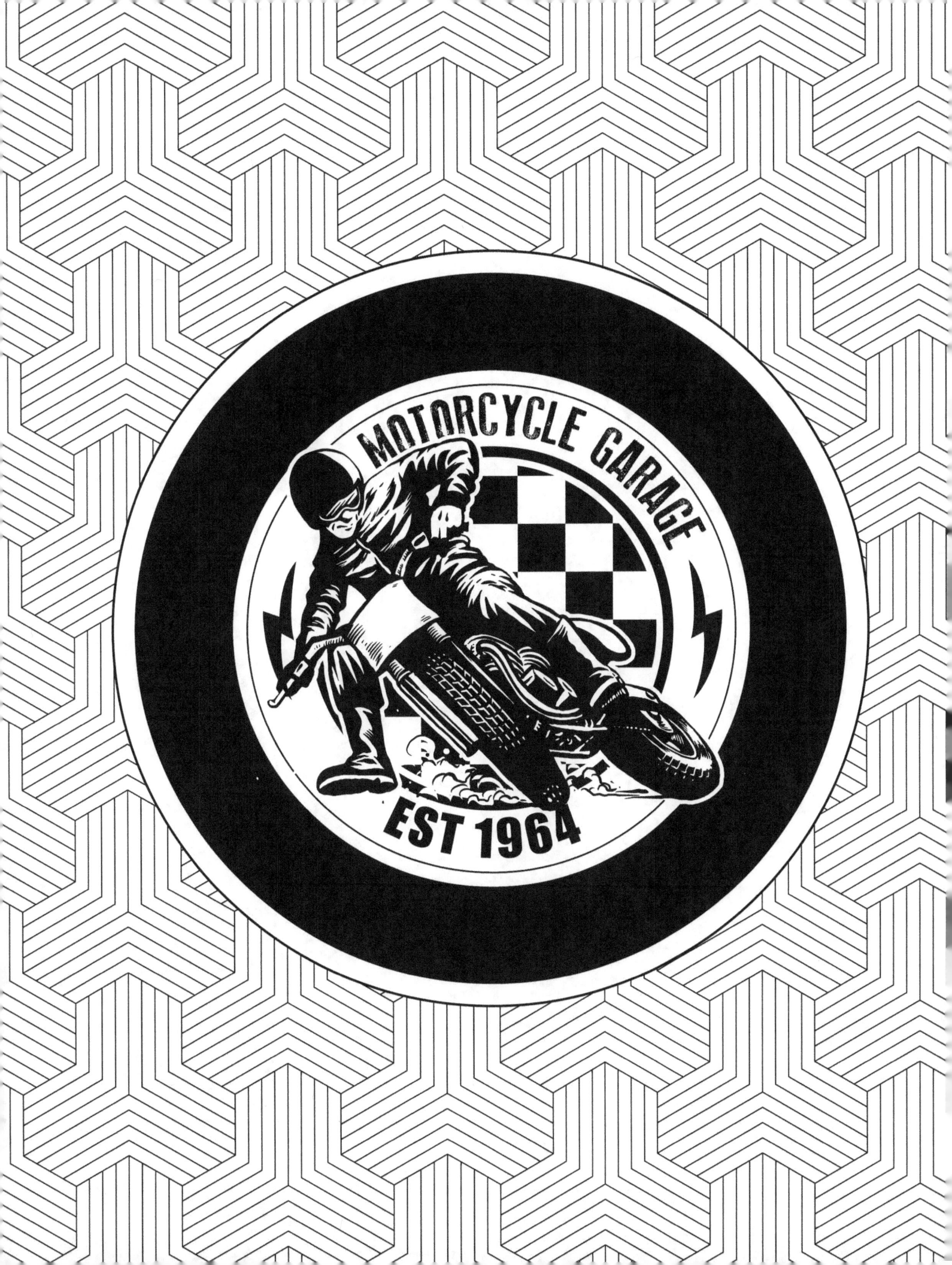

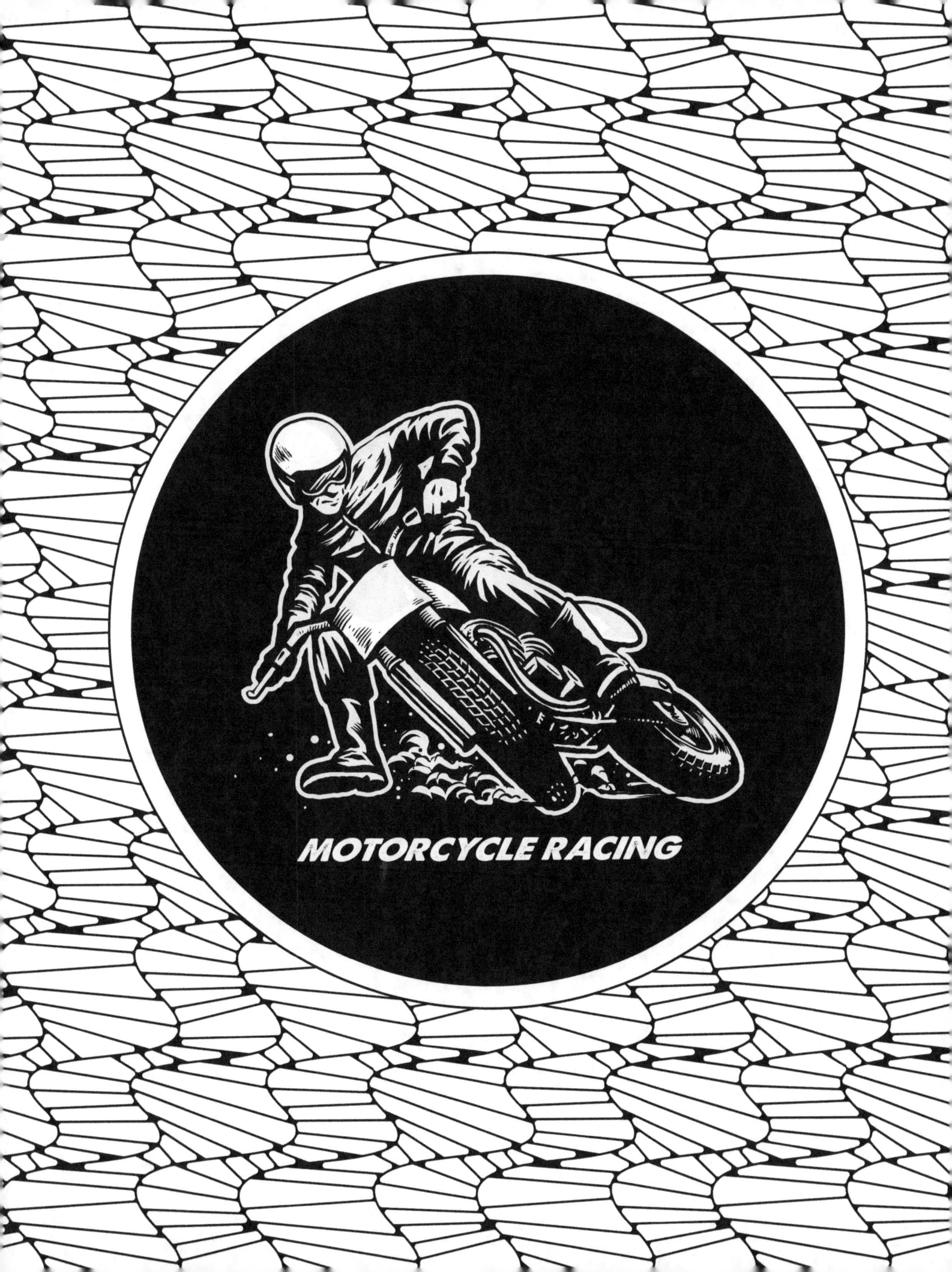

MOTORCYCLE RACING

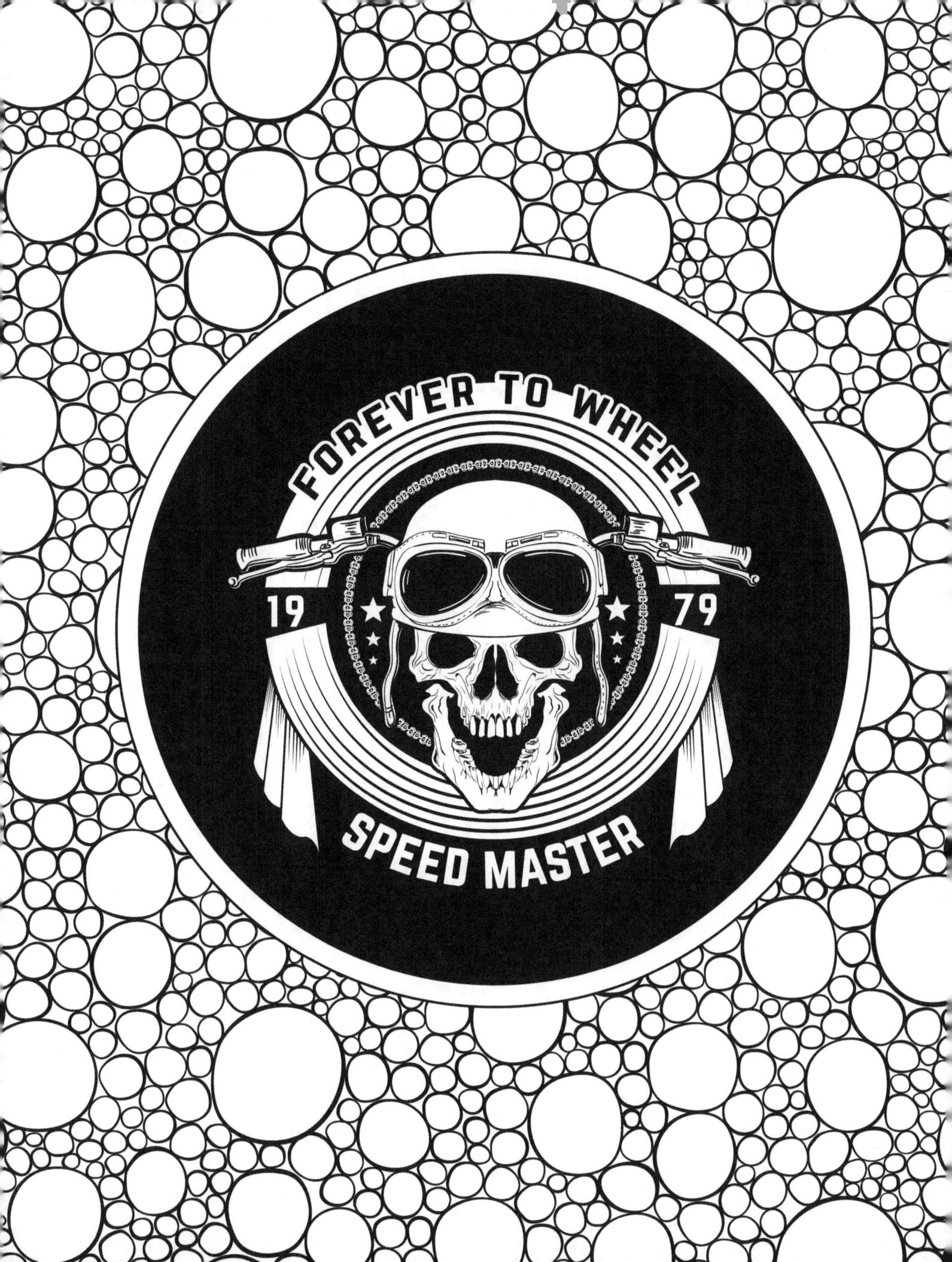

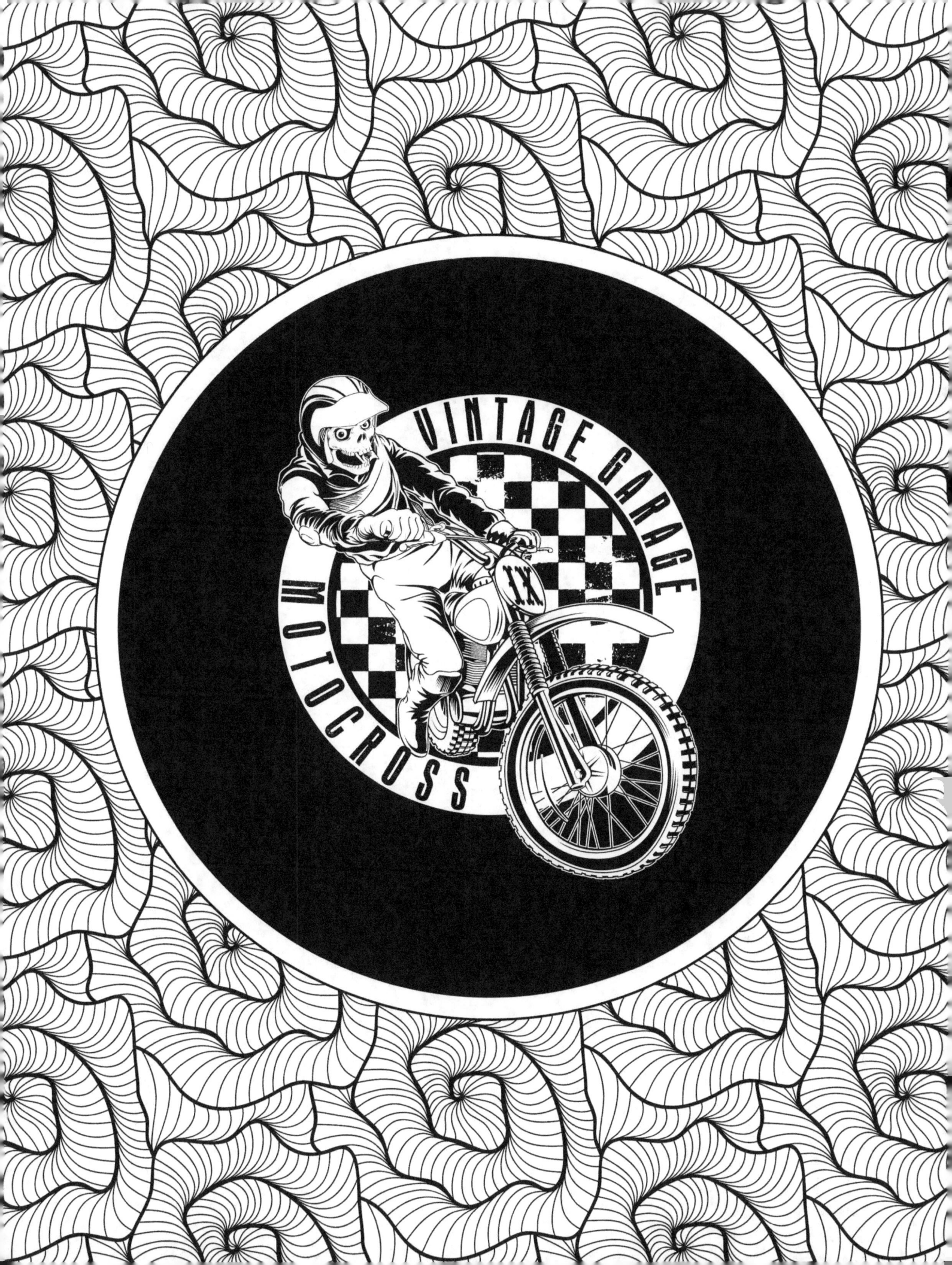

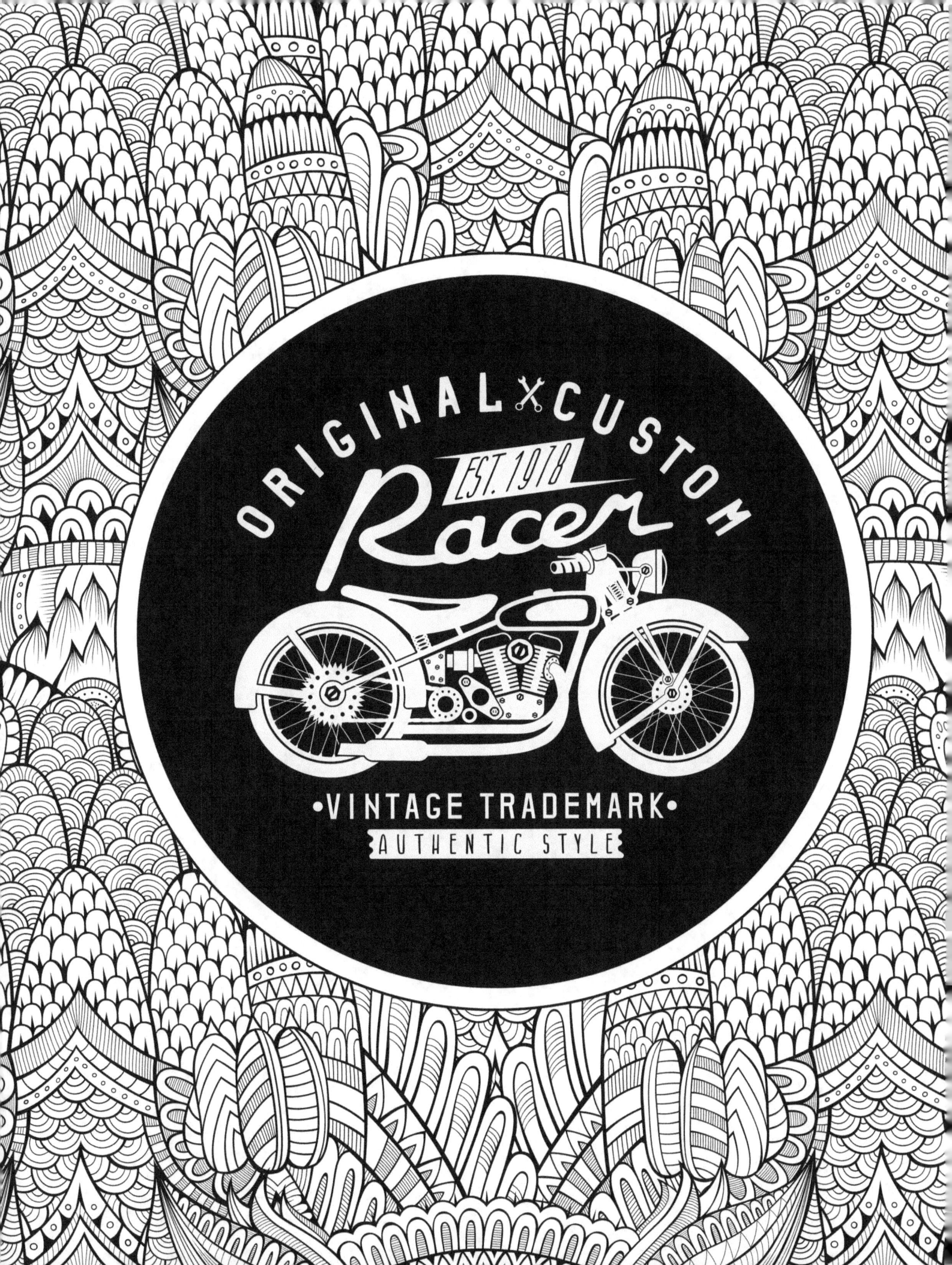

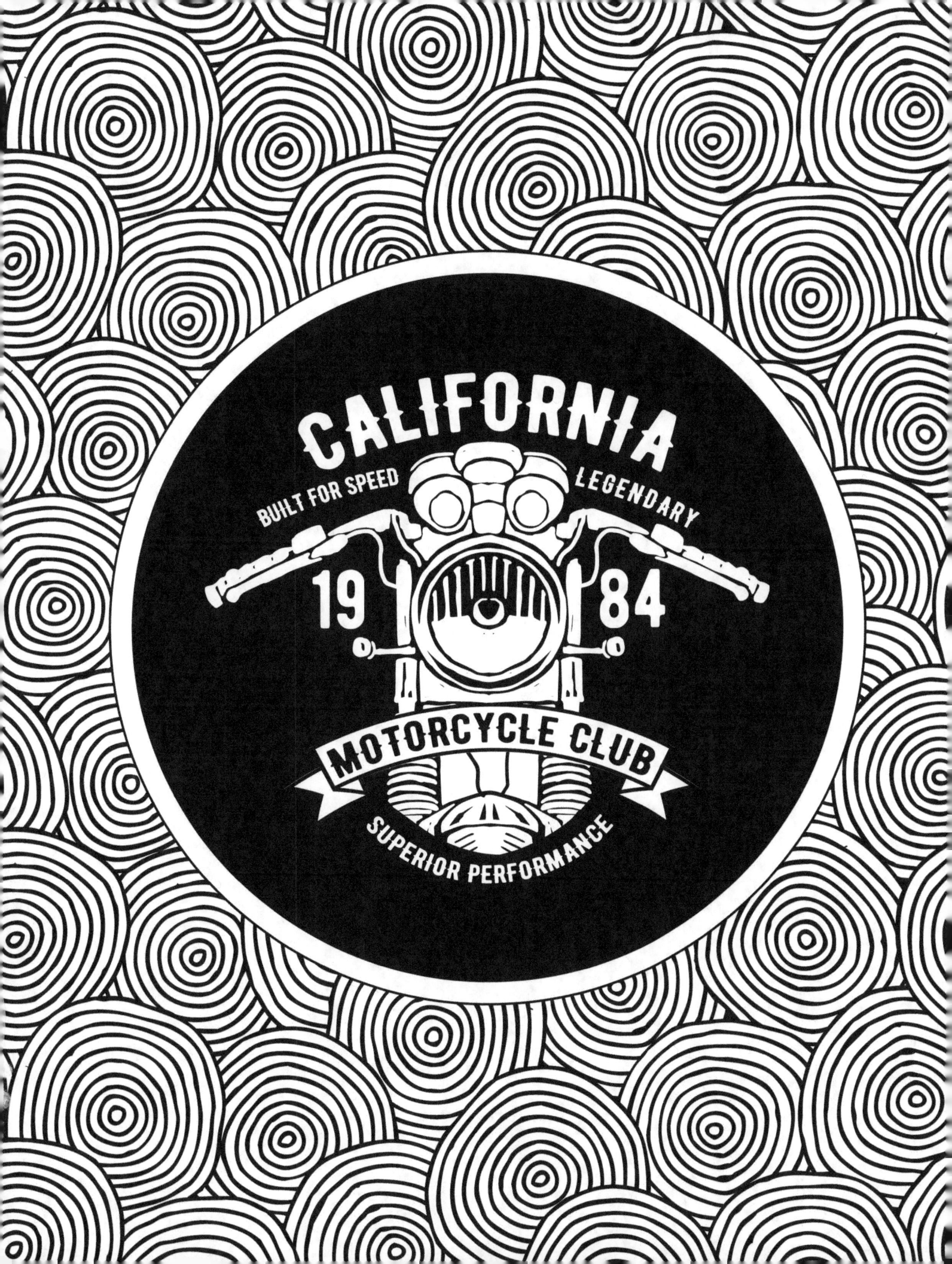

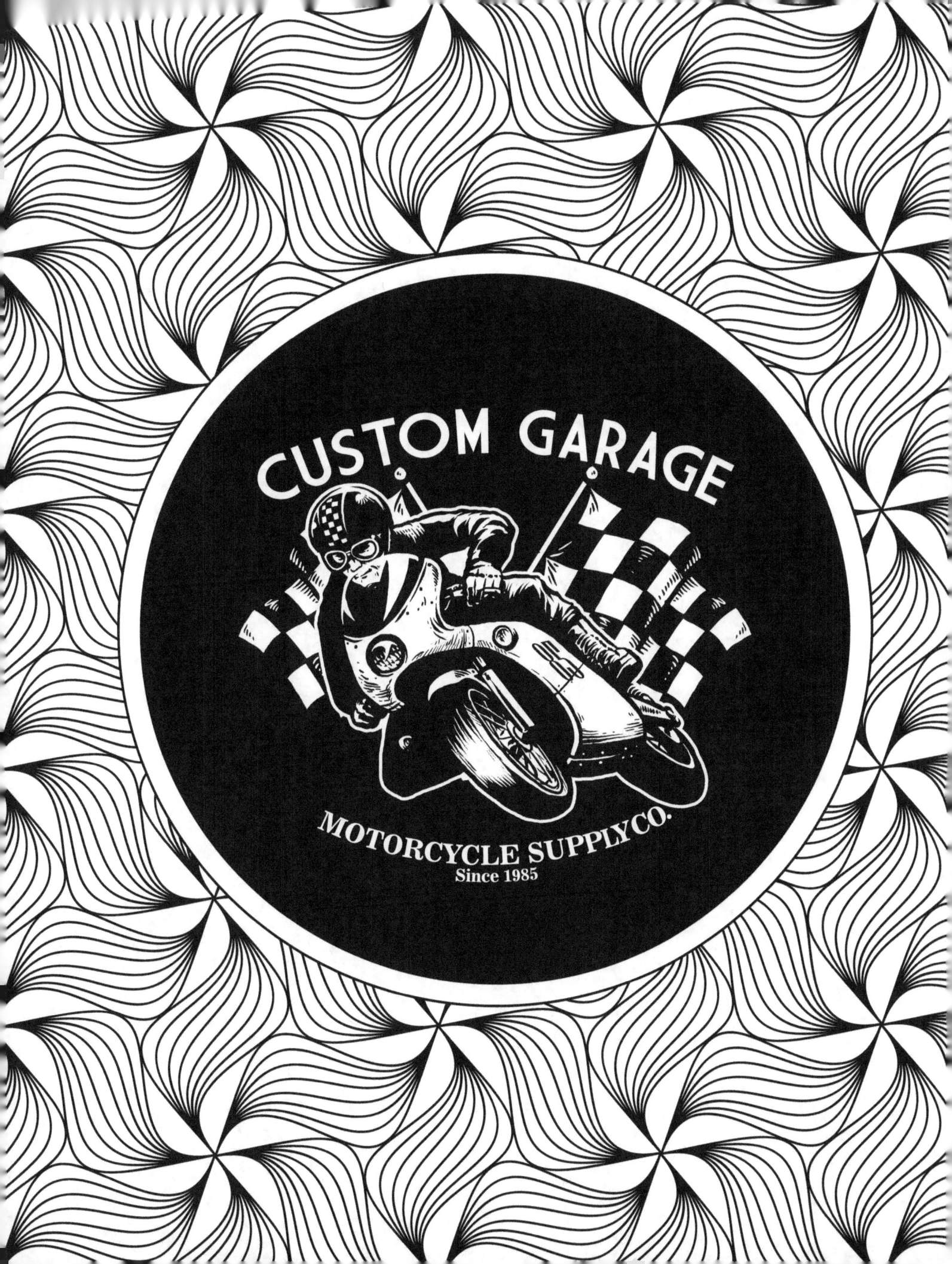

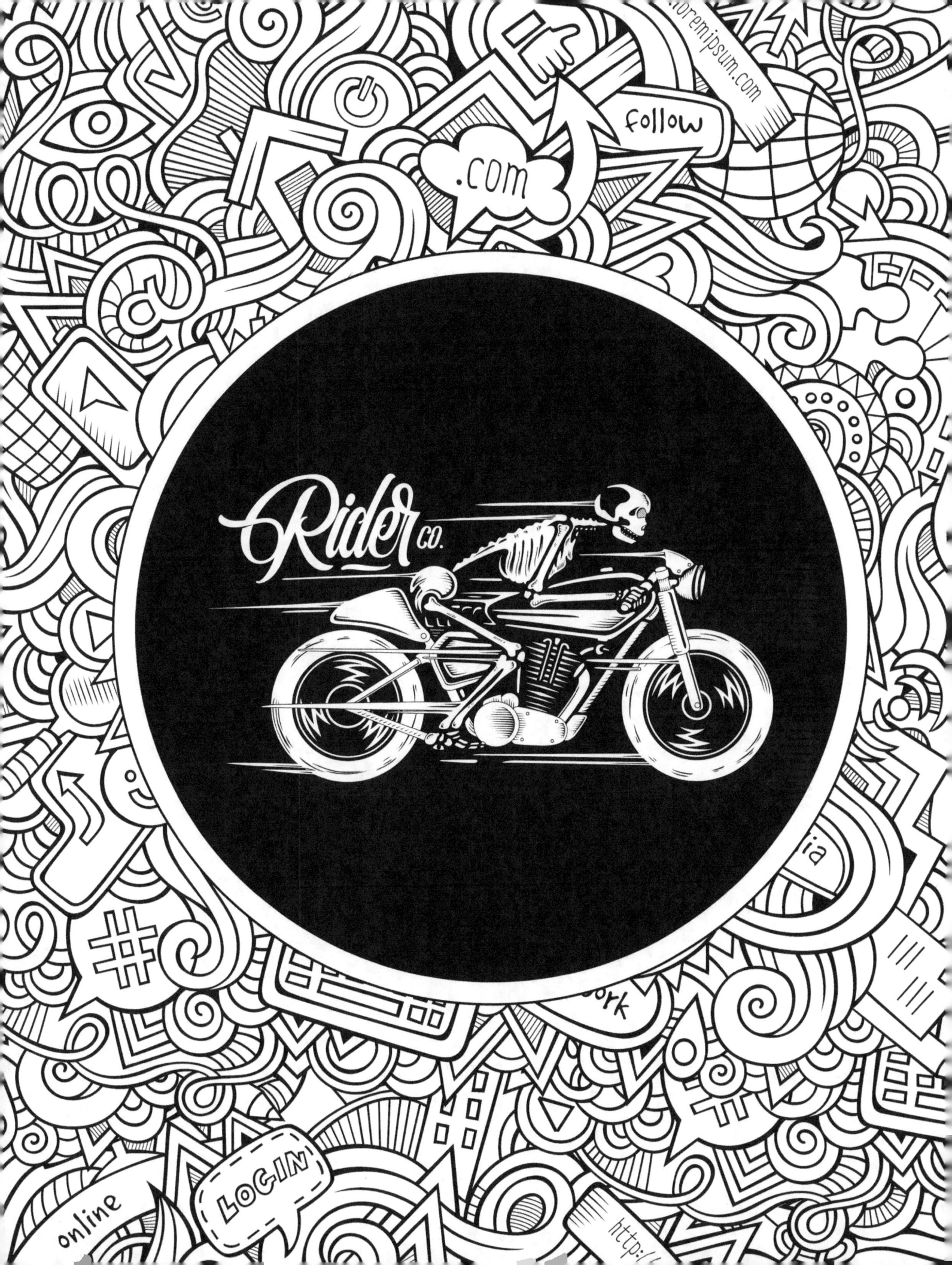

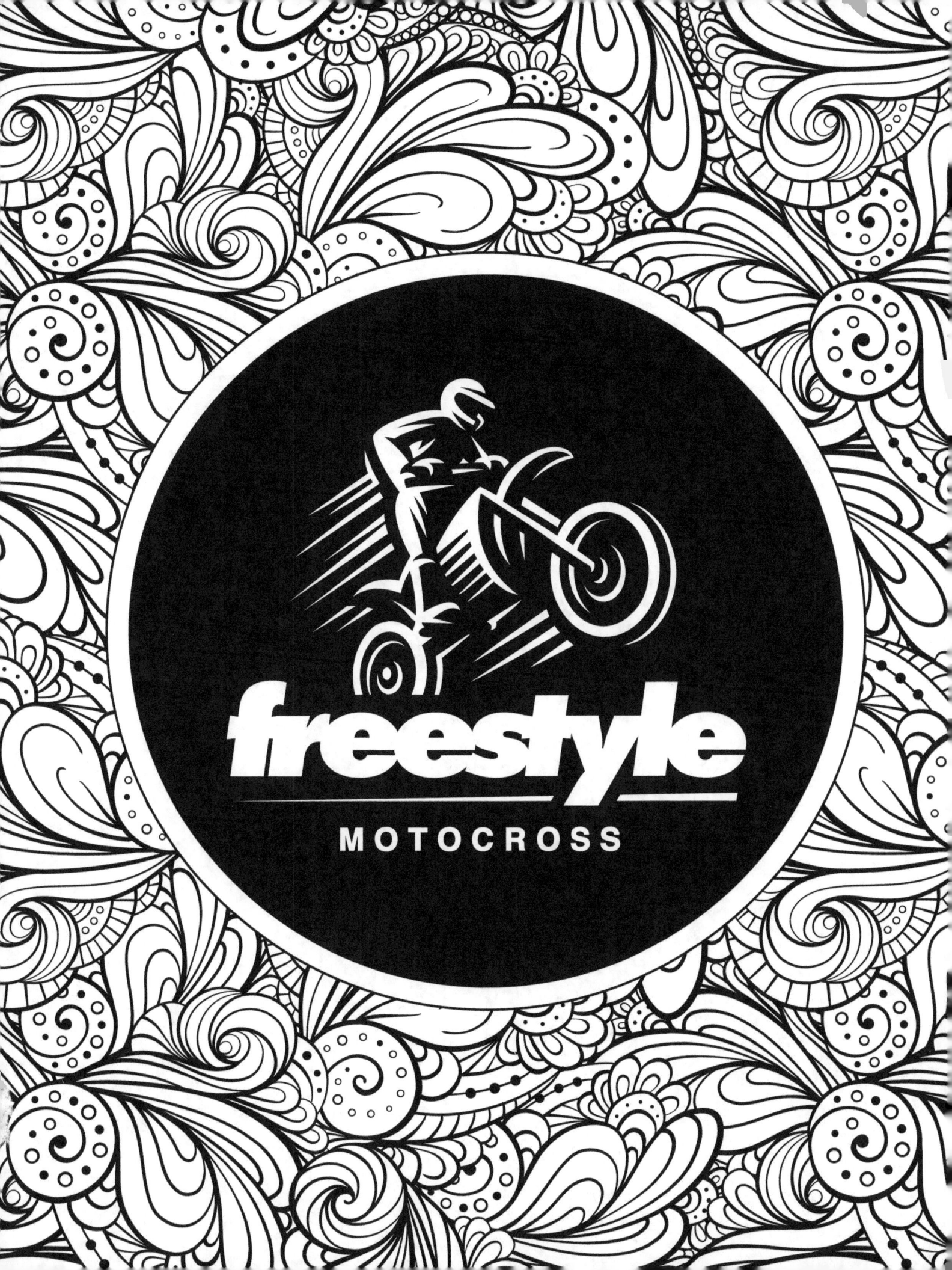

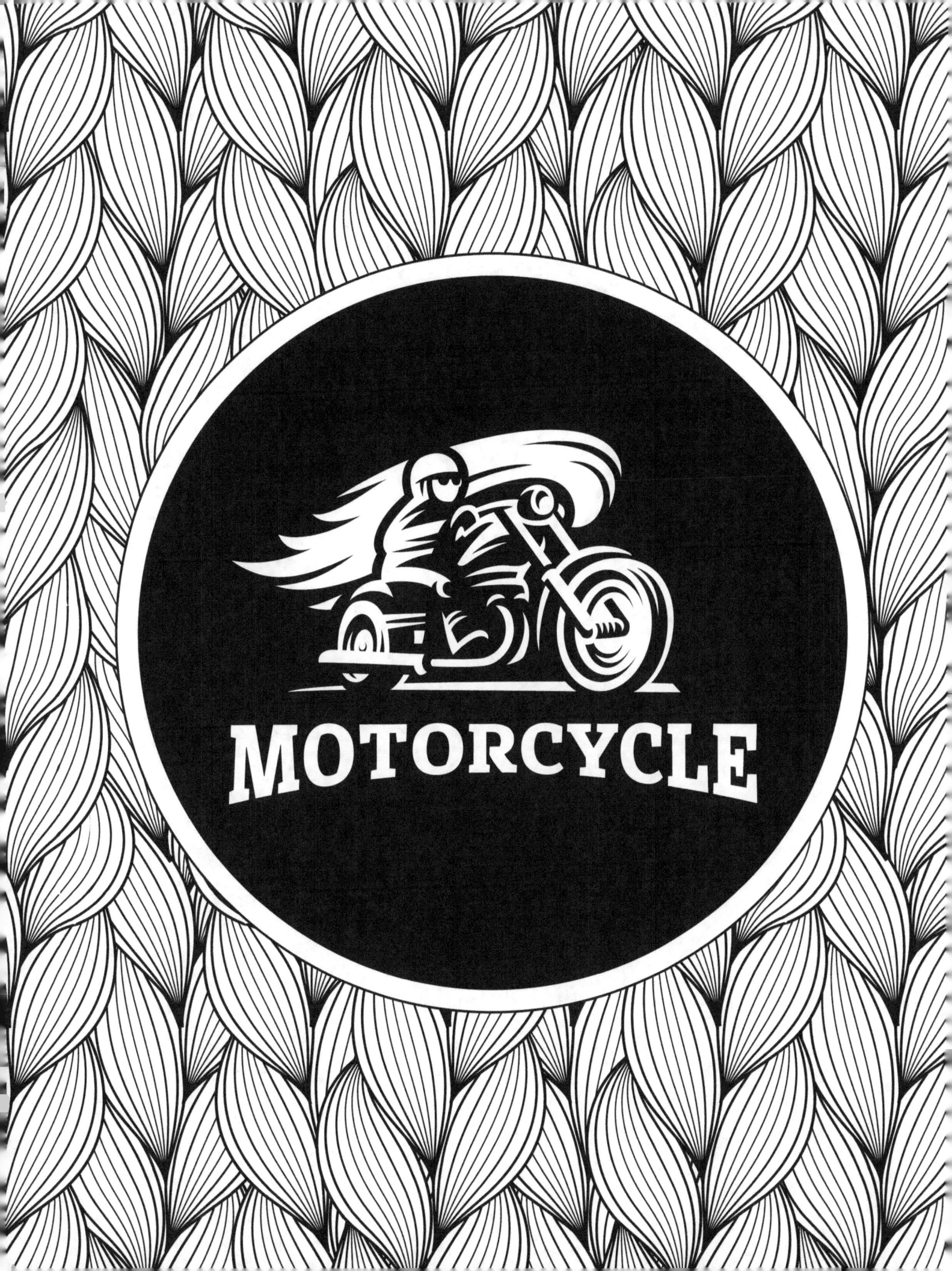

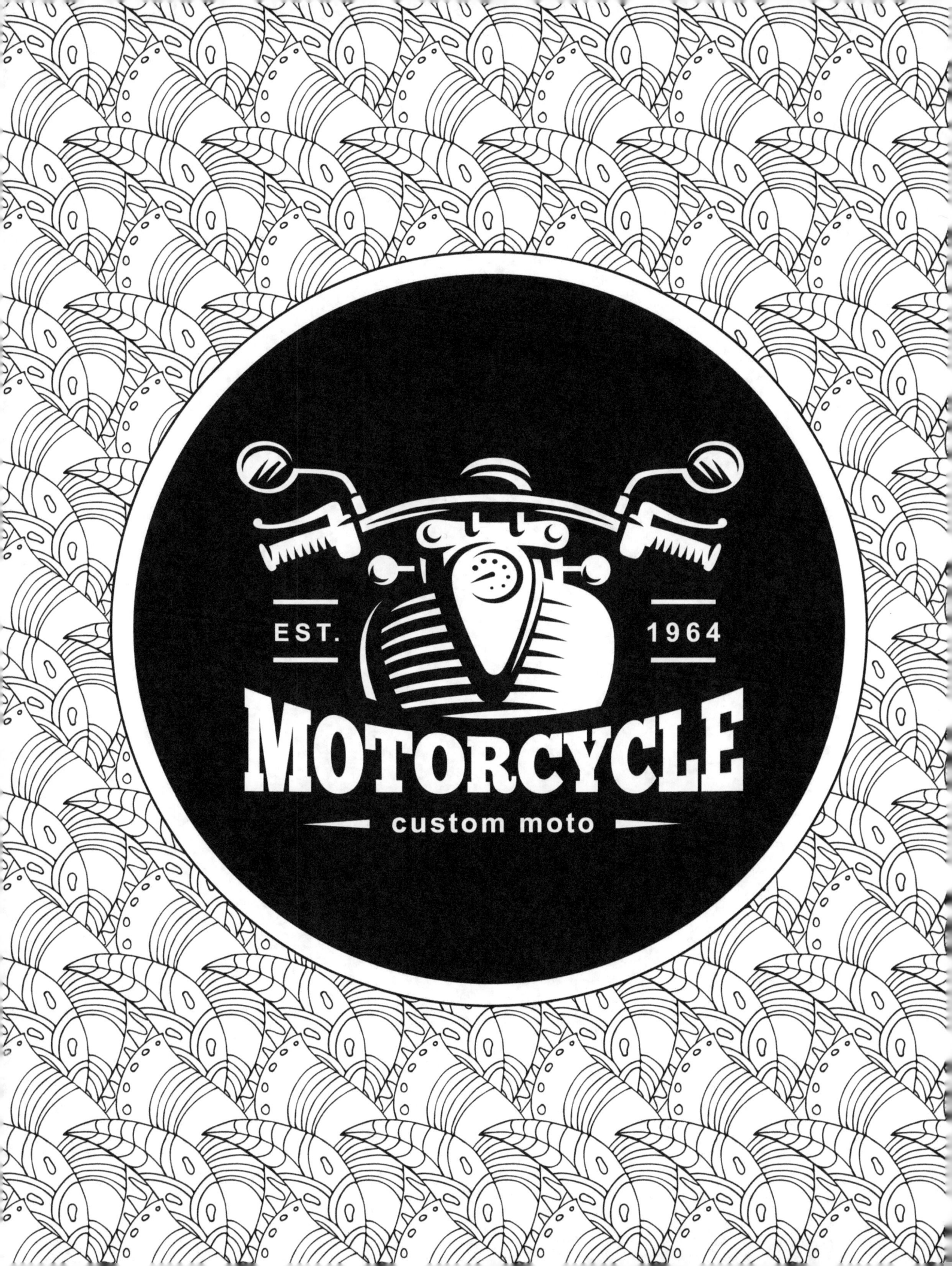

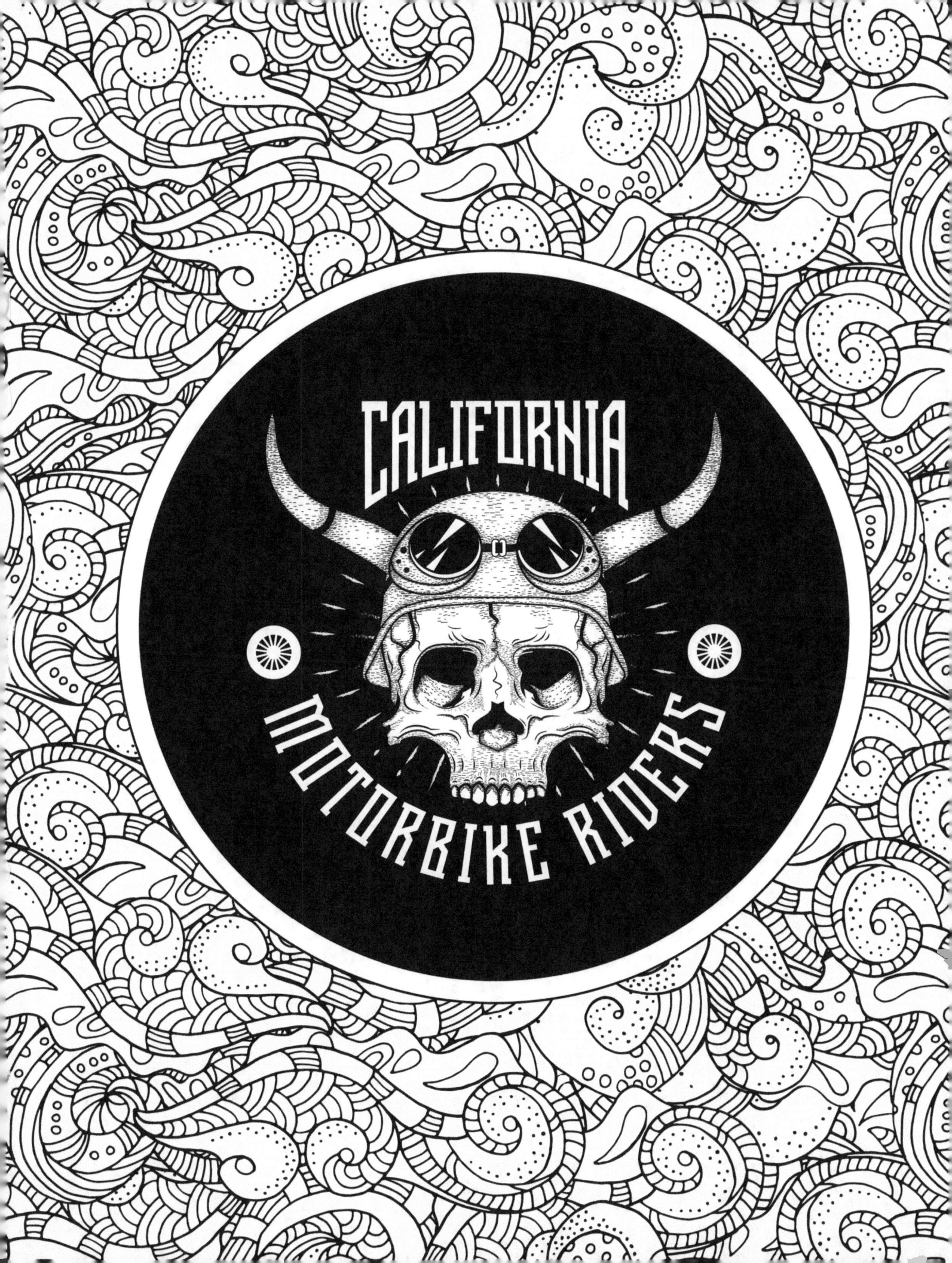

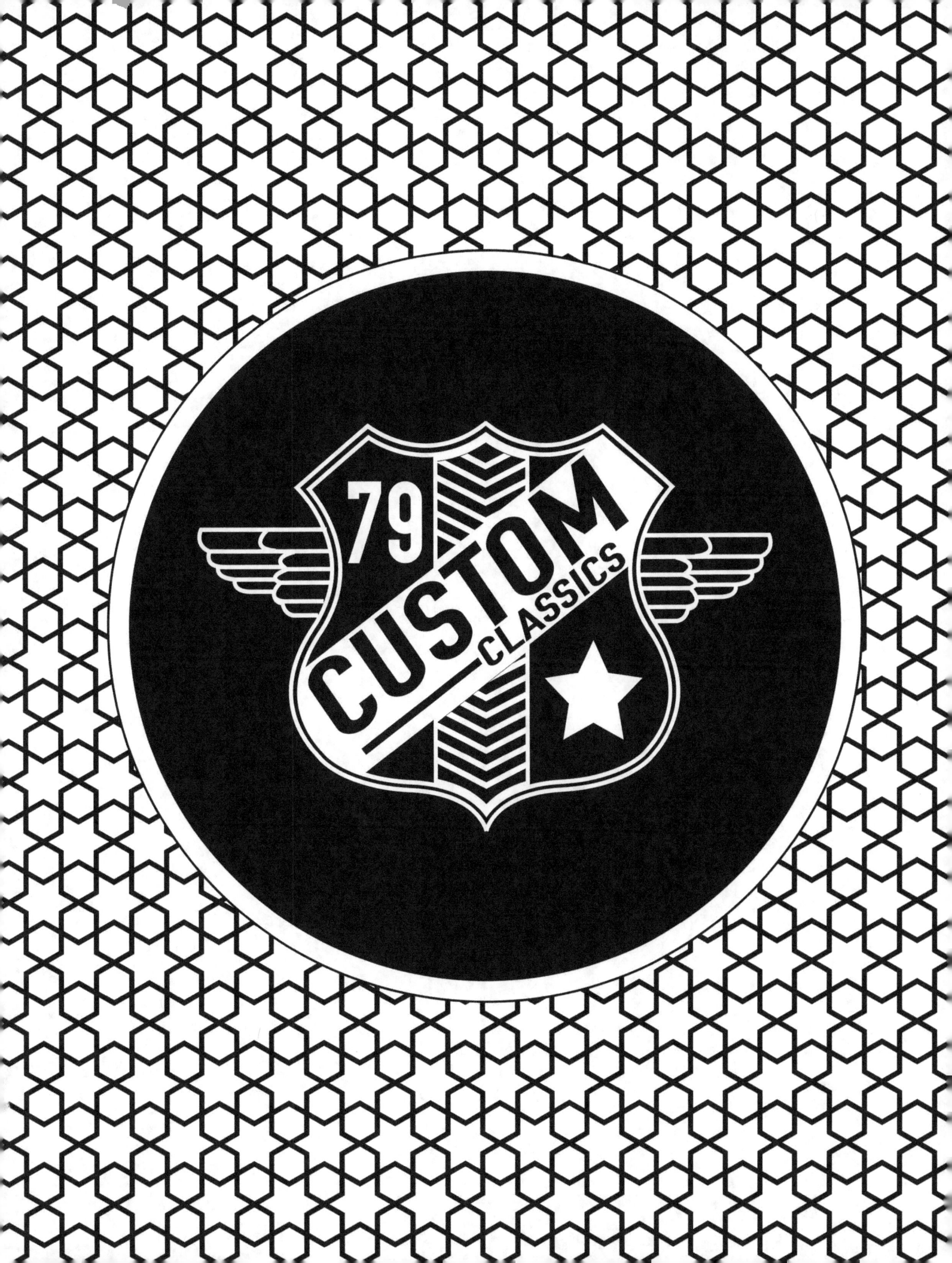

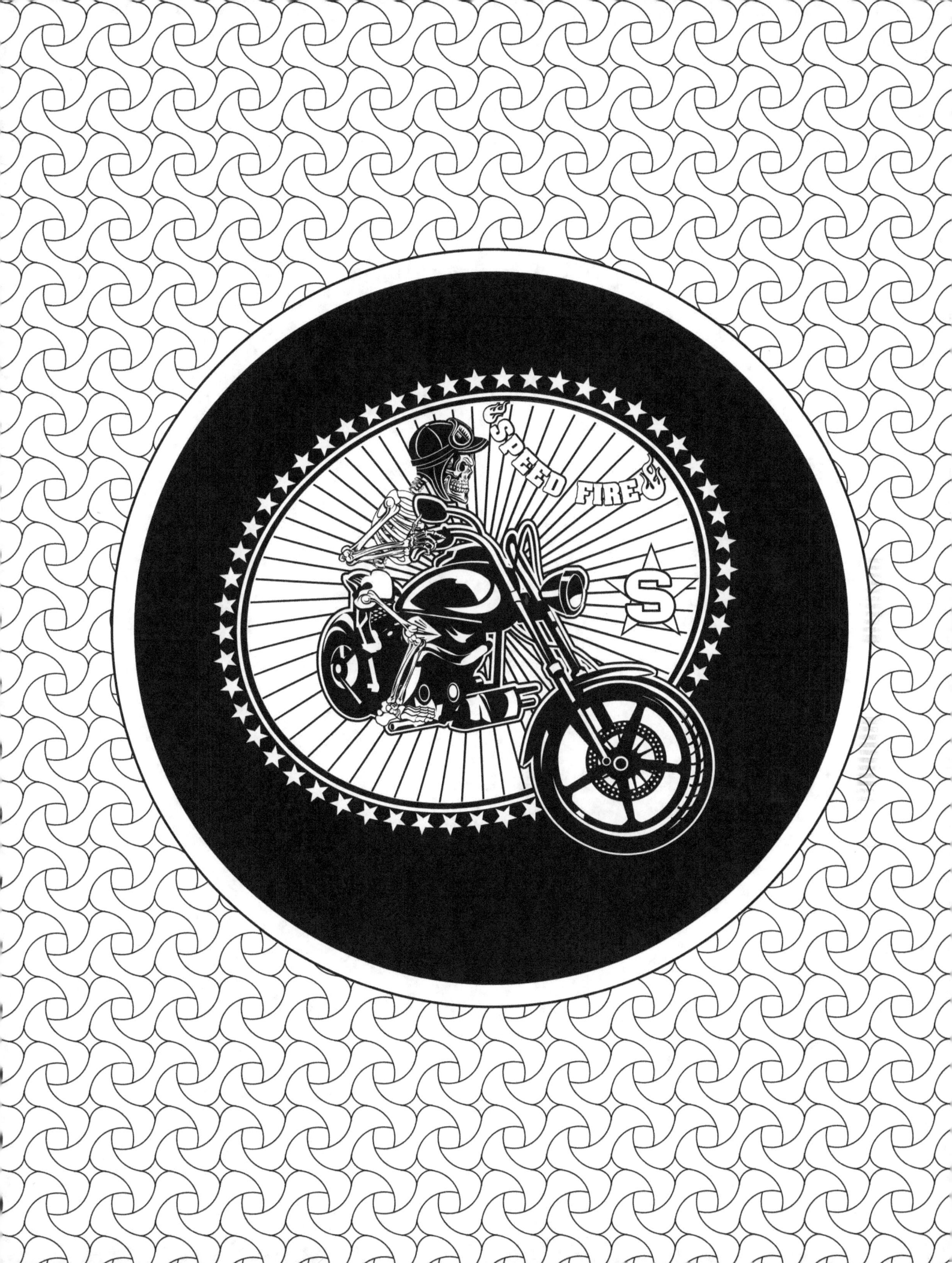

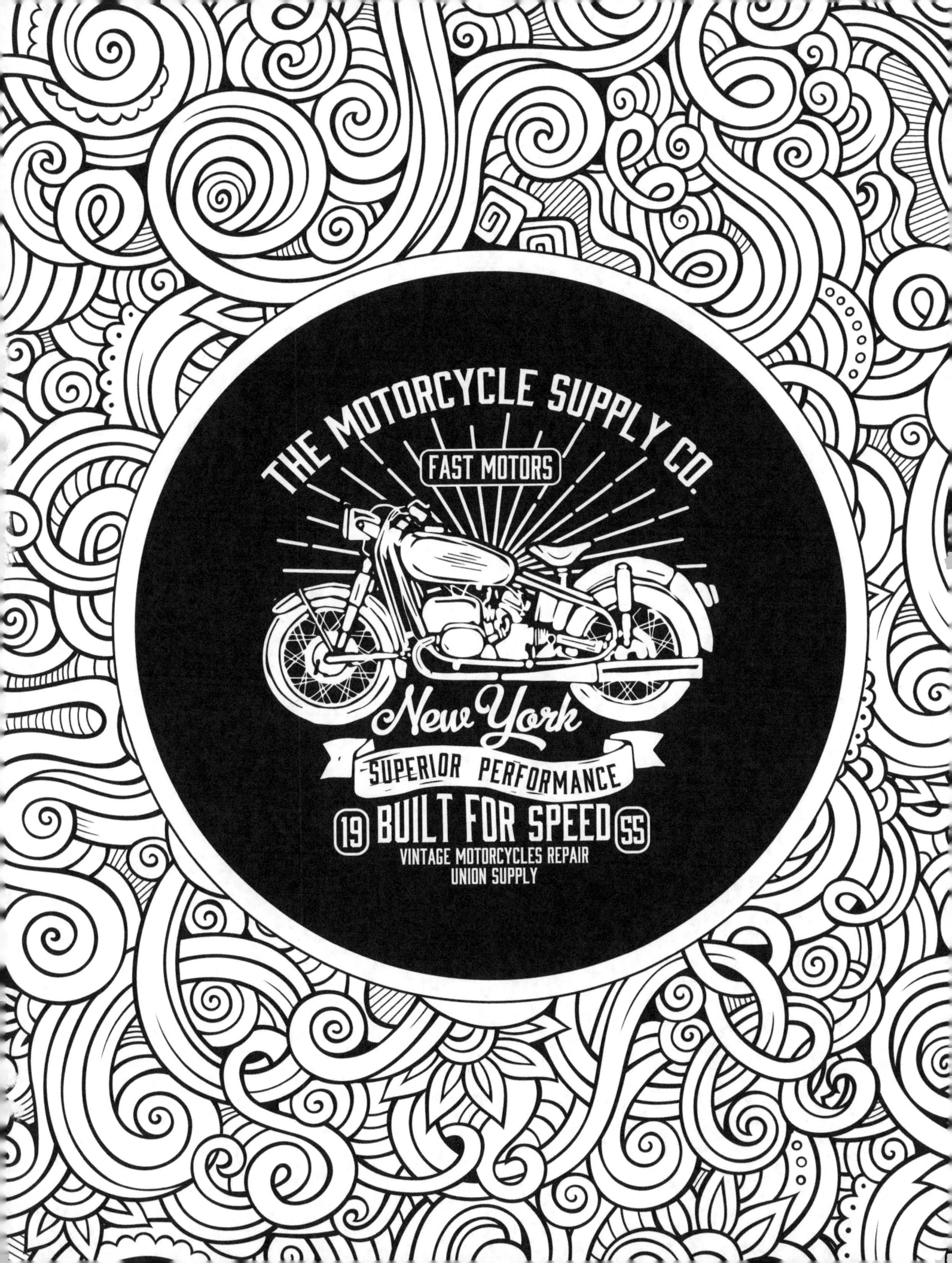

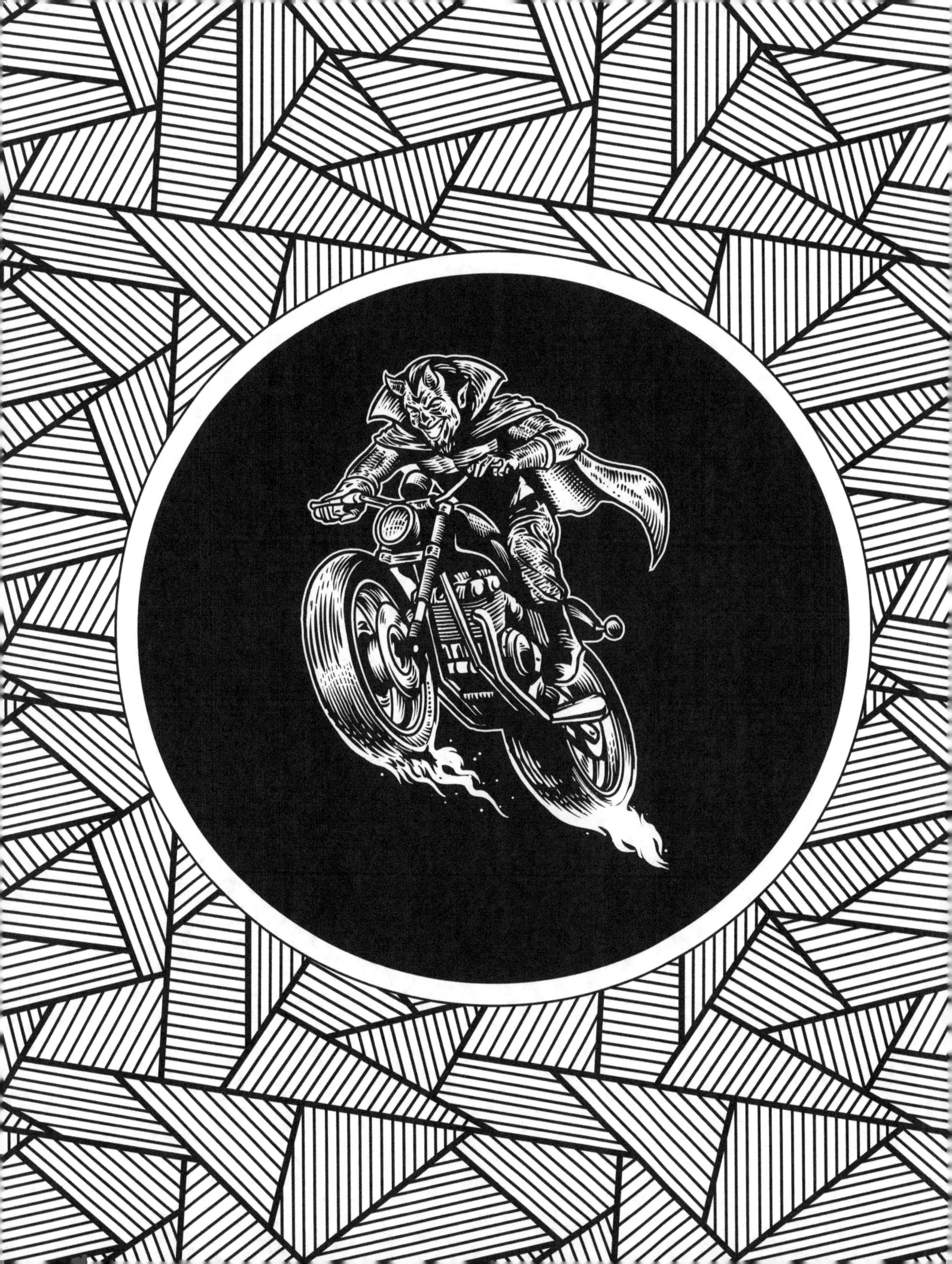

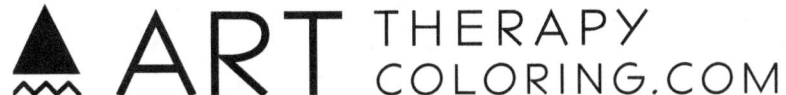

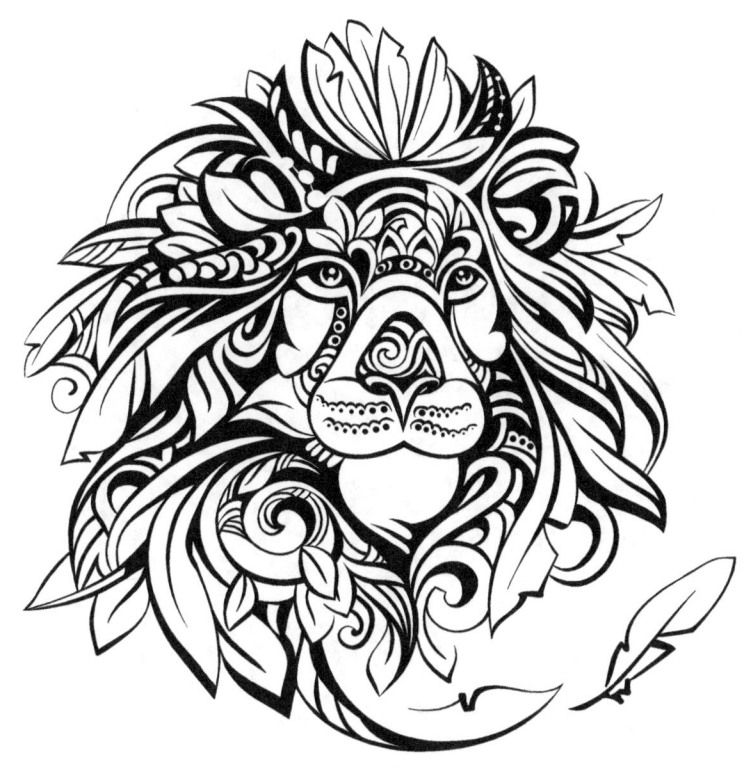

Did You Enjoy Our Coloring Book?

We Want To Hear About It!

Help spread the word about our coloring books! The best way to spread the word is through reviews. We know how busy you are, especially with all of that coloring, but we would appreciate it!

Visit our website at www.arttherapycoloring.com

Over 200 Art Therapy Coloring Books

See our collection of over 200 Art Therapy Coloring Books for Adults, Men, Women, Seniors, Teens, Kids, Boys, and Girls.

Coloring Books For Teens

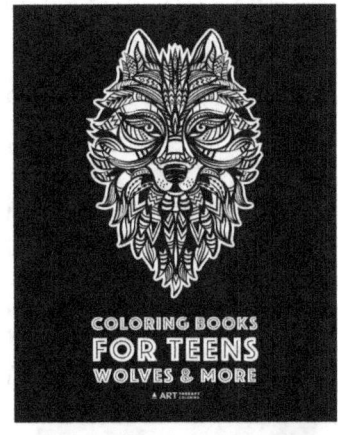

COLORING BOOKS
FOR TEENS
WOLVES & MORE

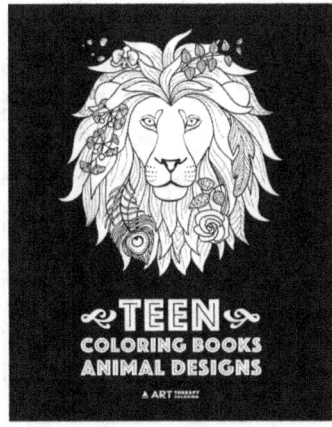

TEEN
COLORING BOOKS
ANIMAL DESIGNS

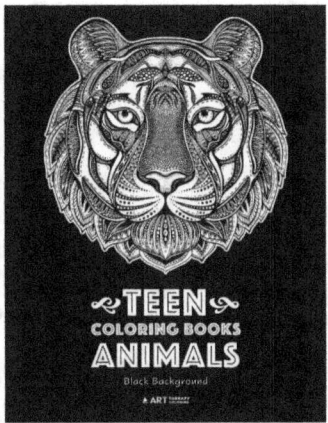

TEEN
COLORING BOOKS
ANIMALS
Black Background

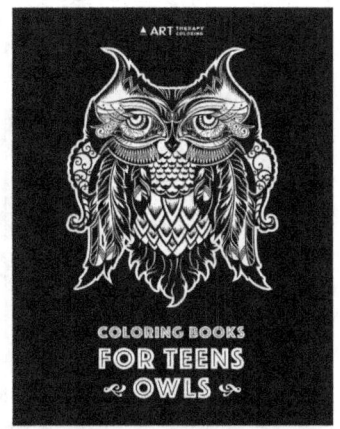

COLORING BOOKS
FOR TEENS
OWLS

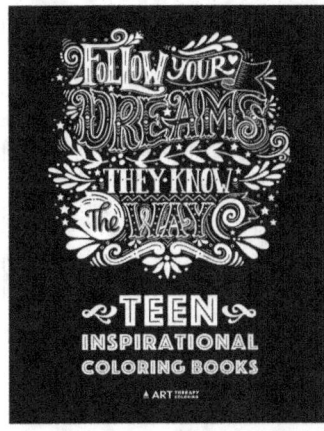

TEEN
INSPIRATIONAL
COLORING BOOKS

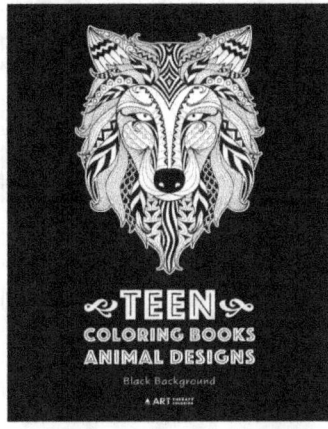

TEEN
COLORING BOOKS
ANIMAL DESIGNS
Black Background

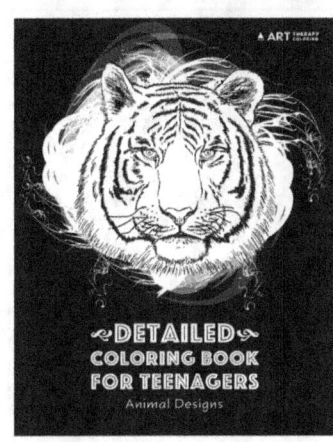

DETAILED
COLORING BOOK
FOR TEENAGERS
Animal Designs

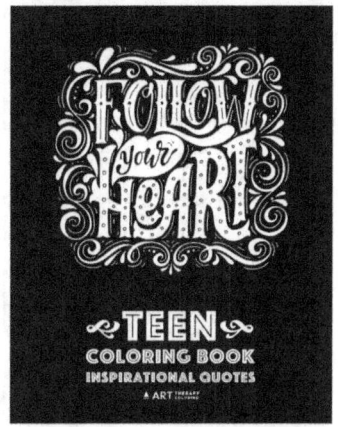

TEEN
COLORING BOOK
INSPIRATIONAL QUOTES

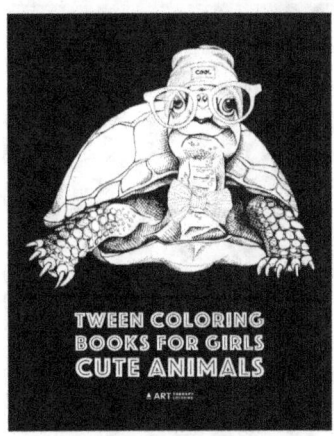

TWEEN COLORING
BOOKS FOR GIRLS
CUTE ANIMALS

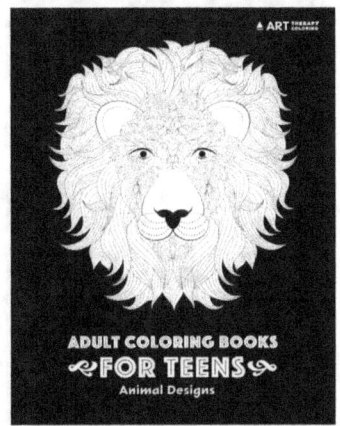

ADULT COLORING BOOKS
FOR TEENS
Animal Designs

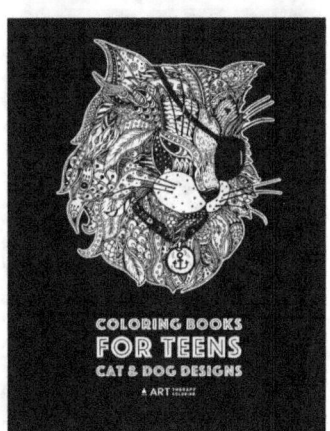

COLORING BOOKS
FOR TEENS
CAT & DOG DESIGNS

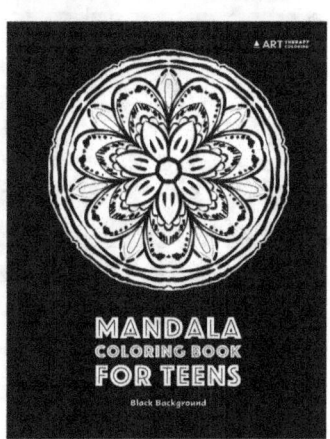

MANDALA
COLORING BOOK
FOR TEENS
Black Background

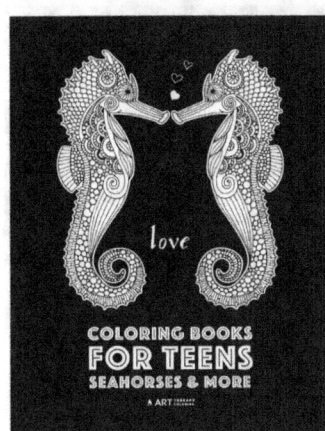

COLORING BOOKS
FOR TEENS
SEAHORSES & MORE

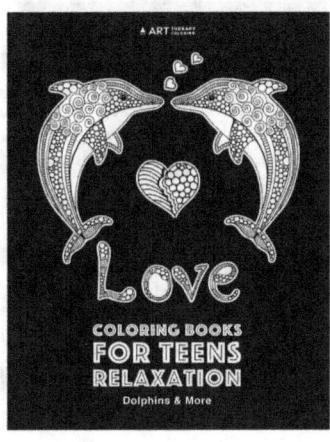

COLORING BOOKS
FOR TEENS
RELAXATION
Dolphins & More

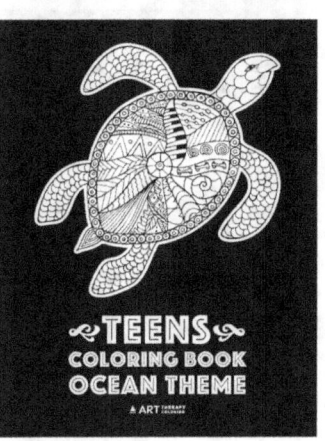

TEENS
COLORING BOOK
OCEAN THEME

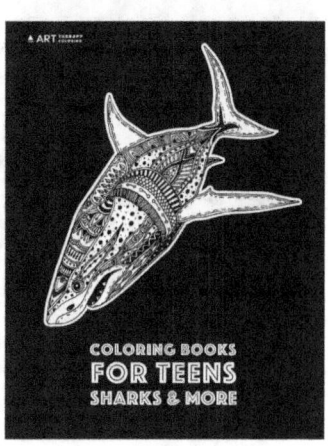

COLORING BOOKS
FOR TEENS
SHARKS & MORE

Coloring Books For Teens

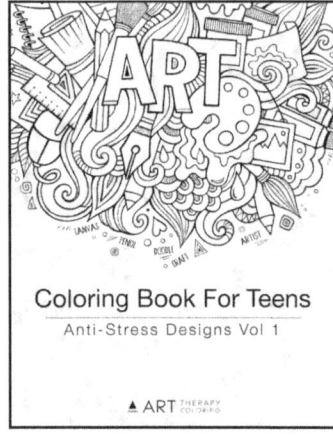

Coloring Book For Teens
Anti-Stress Designs Vol 1

ART THERAPY COLORING

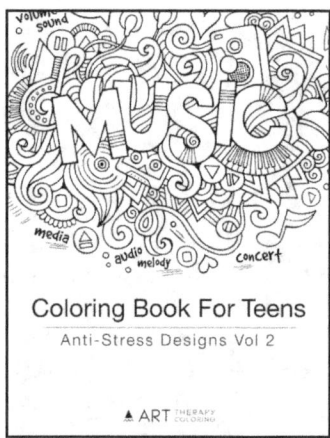

Coloring Book For Teens
Anti-Stress Designs Vol 2

ART THERAPY COLORING

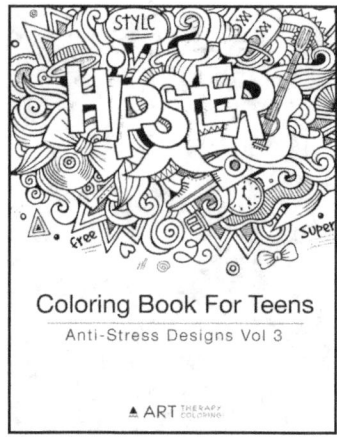

Coloring Book For Teens
Anti-Stress Designs Vol 3

ART THERAPY COLORING

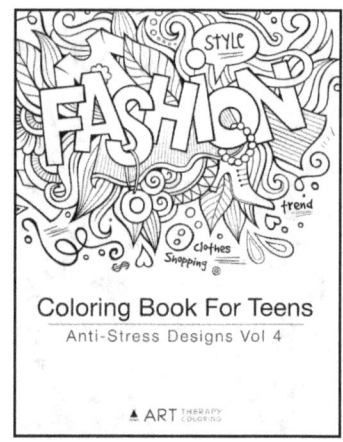

Coloring Book For Teens
Anti-Stress Designs Vol 4

ART THERAPY COLORING

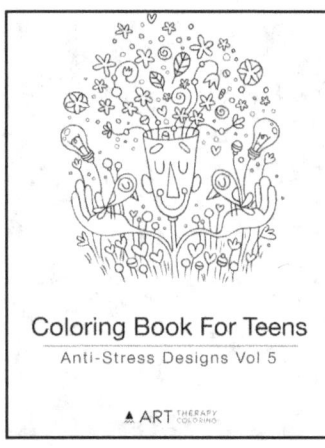

Coloring Book For Teens
Anti-Stress Designs Vol 5

ART THERAPY COLORING

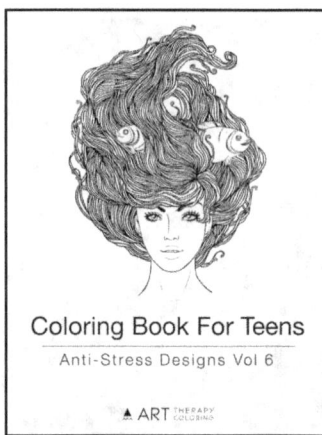

Coloring Book For Teens
Anti-Stress Designs Vol 6

ART THERAPY COLORING

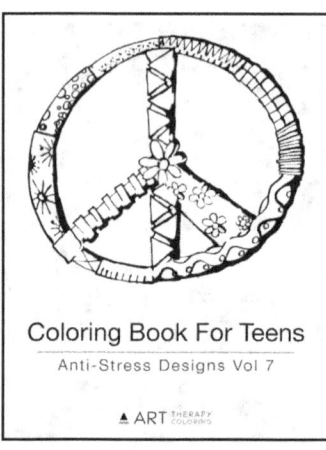

Coloring Book For Teens
Anti-Stress Designs Vol 7

ART THERAPY COLORING

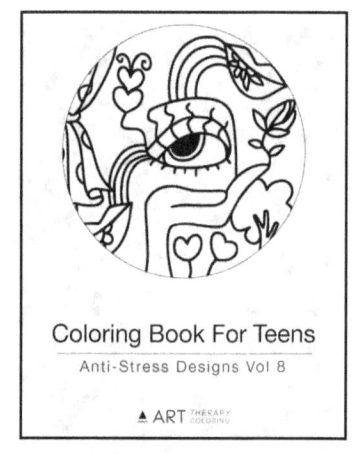

Coloring Book For Teens
Anti-Stress Designs Vol 8

ART THERAPY COLORING

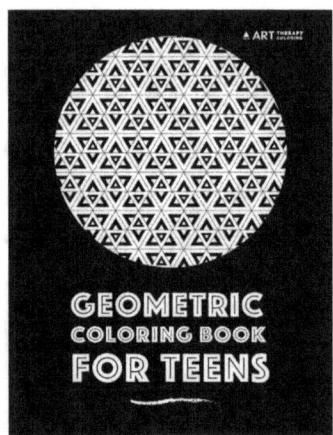

GEOMETRIC COLORING BOOK FOR TEENS

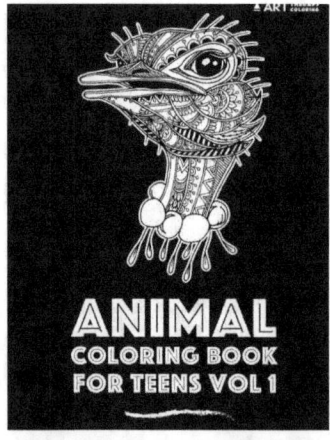

ANIMAL COLORING BOOK FOR TEENS VOL 1

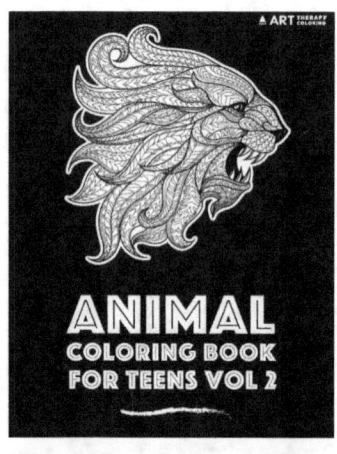

ANIMAL COLORING BOOK FOR TEENS VOL 2

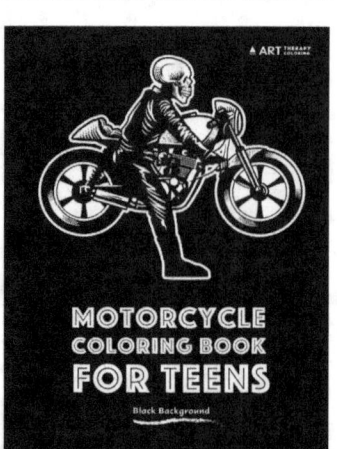

MOTORCYCLE COLORING BOOK FOR TEENS
Black Background

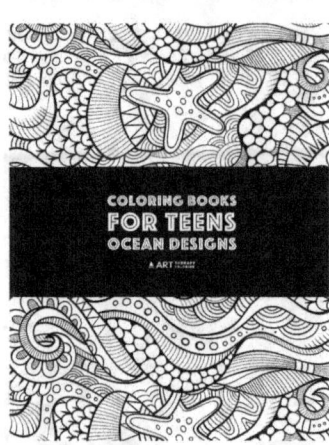

COLORING BOOKS FOR TEENS OCEAN DESIGNS

ART THERAPY COLORING

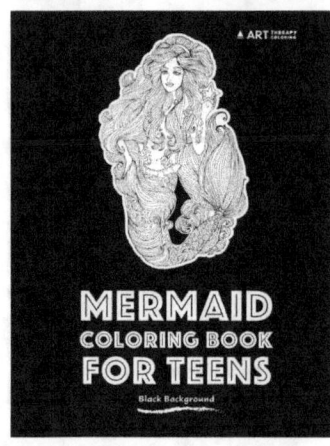

MERMAID COLORING BOOK FOR TEENS
Black Background

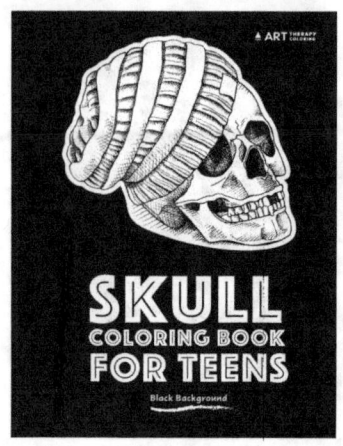

SKULL COLORING BOOK FOR TEENS
Black Background

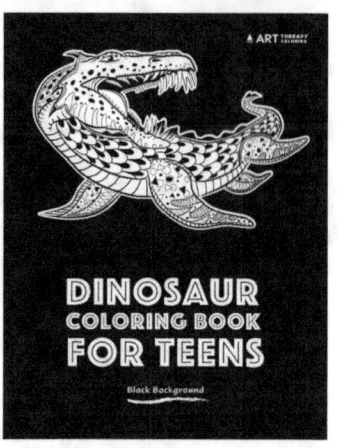

DINOSAUR COLORING BOOK FOR TEENS
Black Background

Coloring Books For Girls

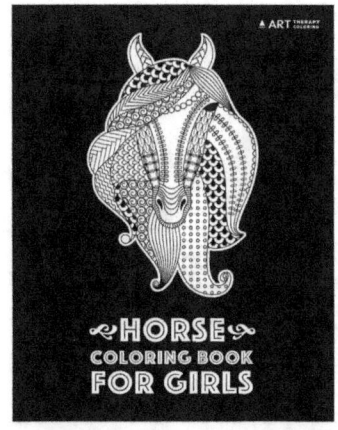

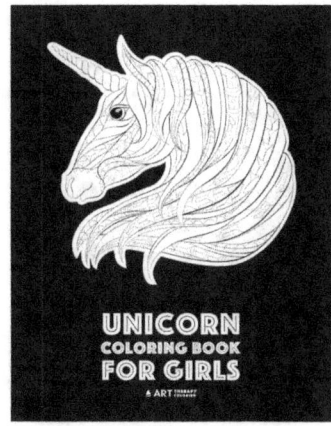

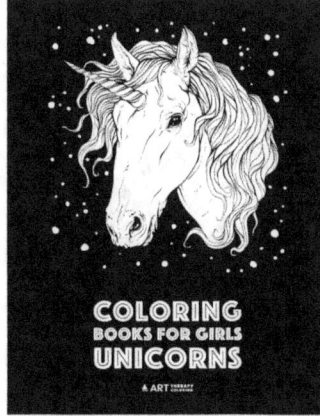

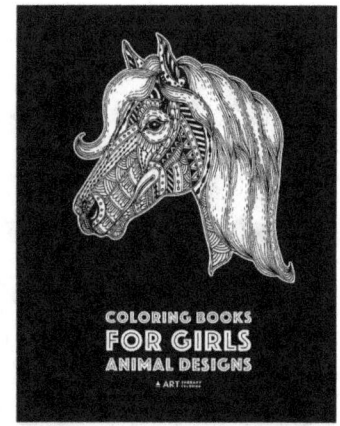

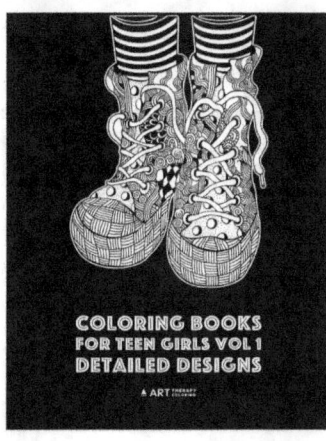

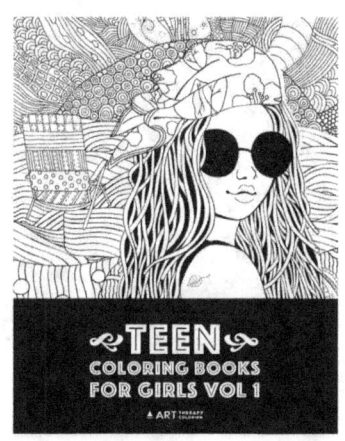

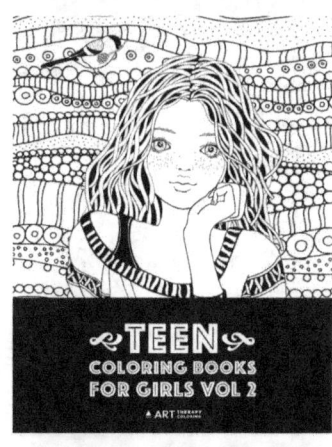

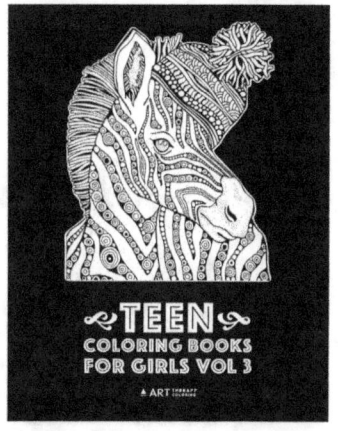

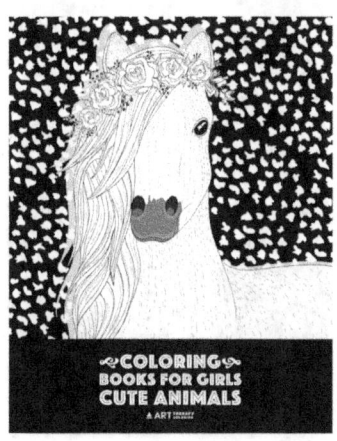

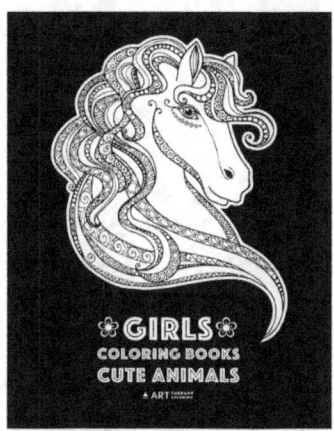

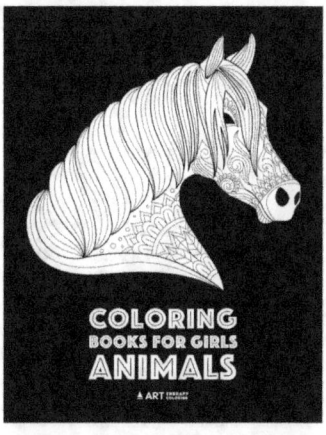

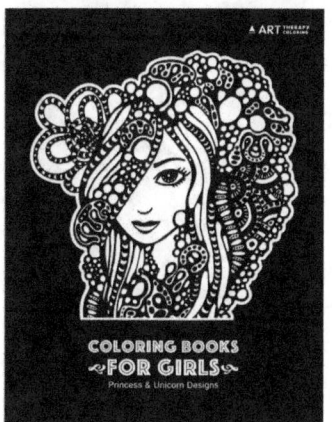

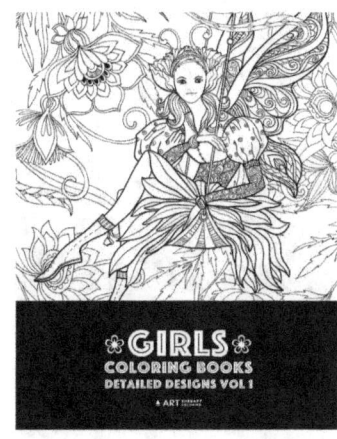

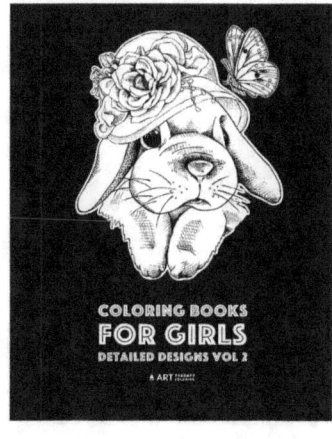

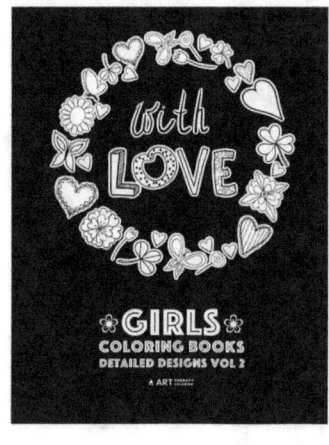

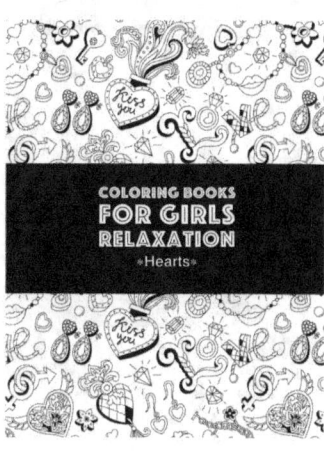

Coloring Books For Boys

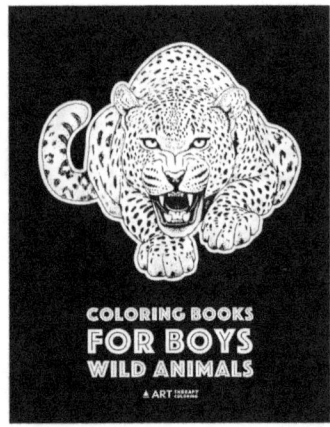

COLORING BOOKS
FOR BOYS
WILD ANIMALS

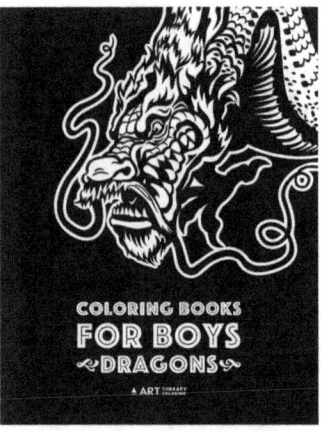

COLORING BOOKS
FOR BOYS
~ DRAGONS ~

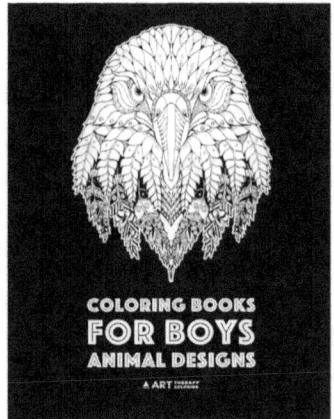

COLORING BOOKS
FOR BOYS
ANIMAL DESIGNS

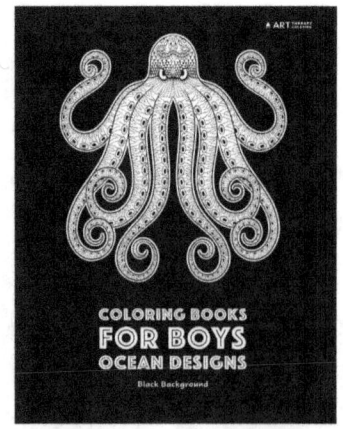

COLORING BOOKS
FOR BOYS
OCEAN DESIGNS
Black Background

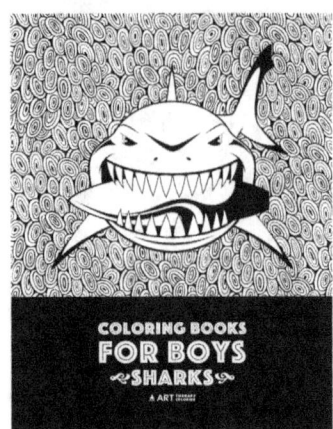

COLORING BOOKS
FOR BOYS
~ SHARKS ~

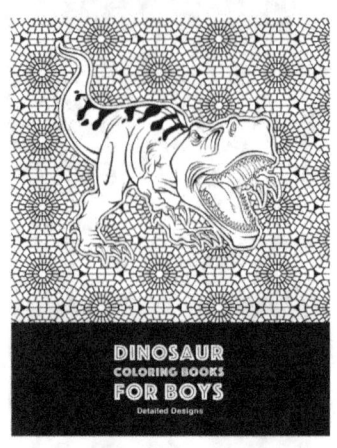

DINOSAUR
COLORING BOOKS
FOR BOYS
Detailed Designs

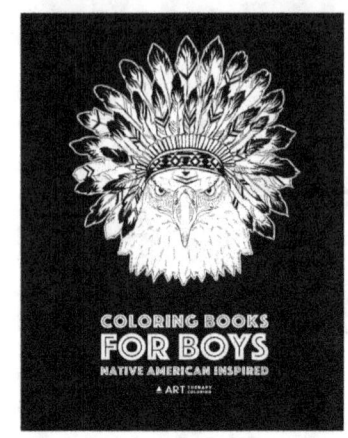

COLORING BOOKS
FOR BOYS
NATIVE AMERICAN INSPIRED

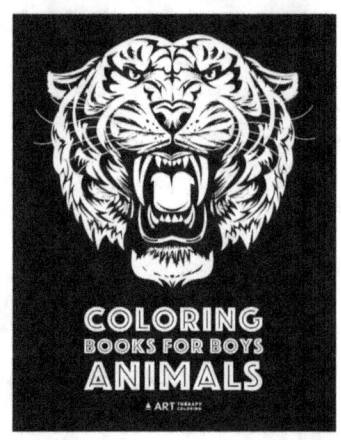

COLORING
BOOKS FOR BOYS
ANIMALS

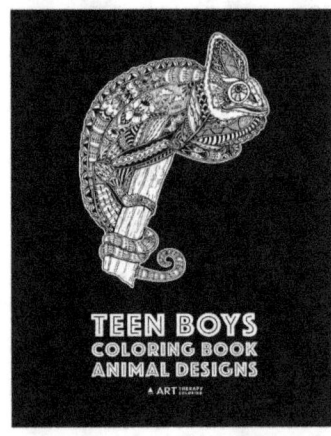

TEEN BOYS
COLORING BOOK
ANIMAL DESIGNS

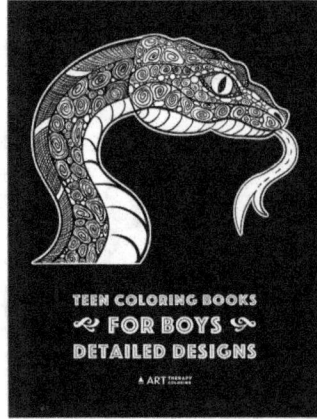

TEEN COLORING BOOKS
~ FOR BOYS ~
DETAILED DESIGNS

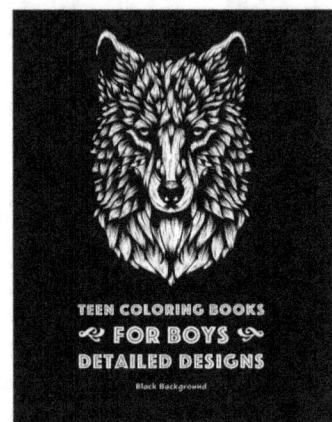

TEEN COLORING BOOKS
~ FOR BOYS ~
DETAILED DESIGNS
Black Background

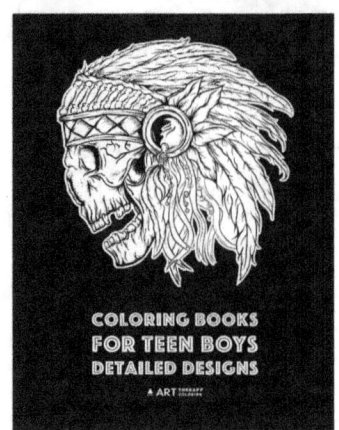

COLORING BOOKS
FOR TEEN BOYS
DETAILED DESIGNS

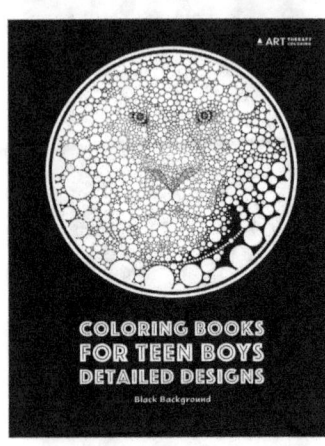

COLORING BOOKS
FOR TEEN BOYS
DETAILED DESIGNS
Black Background

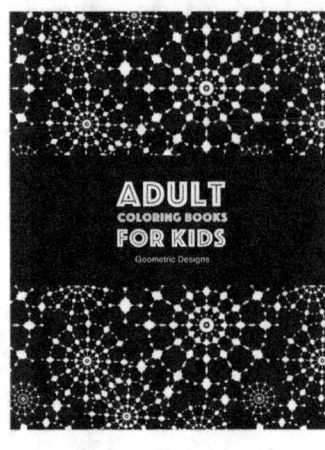

ADULT
COLORING BOOKS
FOR KIDS
Geometric Designs

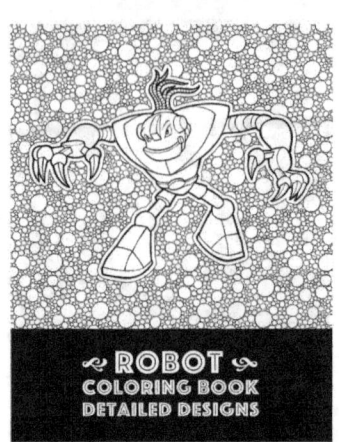

~ ROBOT ~
COLORING BOOK
DETAILED DESIGNS

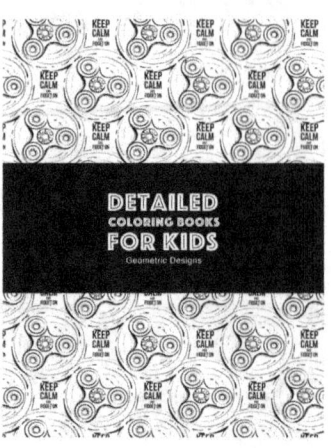

DETAILED
COLORING BOOKS
FOR KIDS
Geometric Designs

Art Therapy Coloring Books

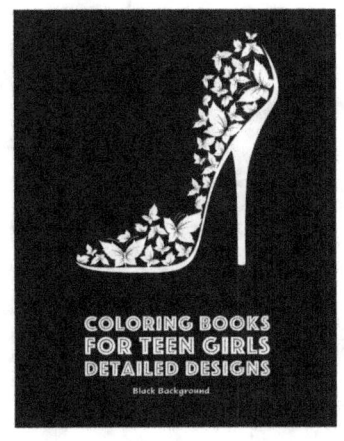

COLORING BOOKS FOR TEEN GIRLS DETAILED DESIGNS
Black Background

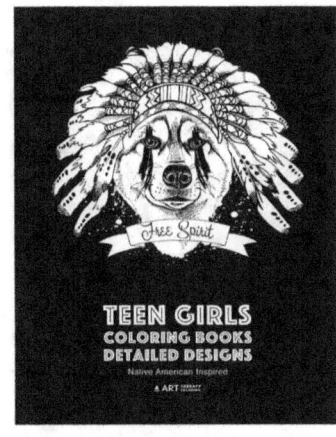

TEEN GIRLS COLORING BOOKS DETAILED DESIGNS
Native American Inspired

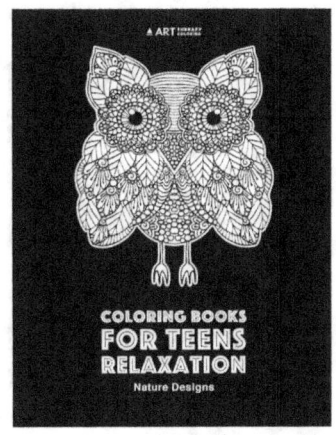

COLORING BOOKS FOR TEENS RELAXATION
Nature Designs

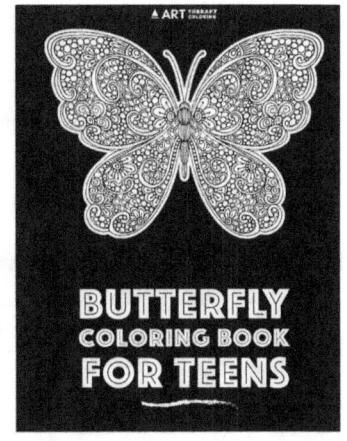

BUTTERFLY COLORING BOOK FOR TEENS

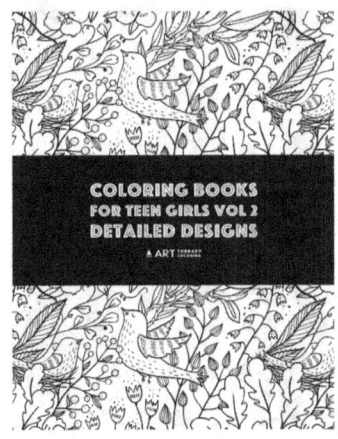

COLORING BOOKS FOR TEEN GIRLS VOL 2 DETAILED DESIGNS

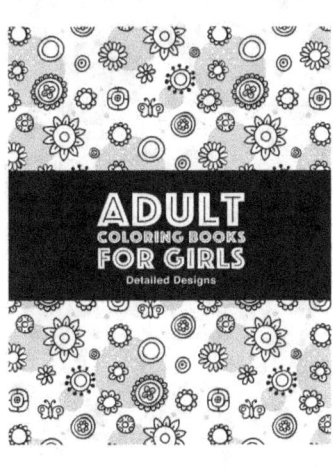

ADULT COLORING BOOKS FOR GIRLS
Detailed Designs

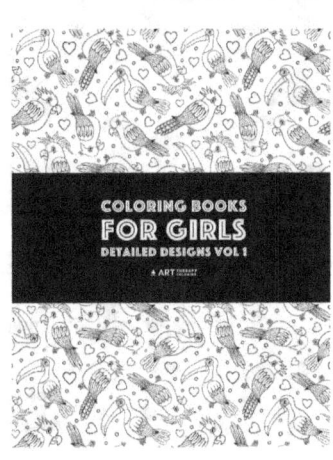

COLORING BOOKS FOR GIRLS DETAILED DESIGNS VOL 1

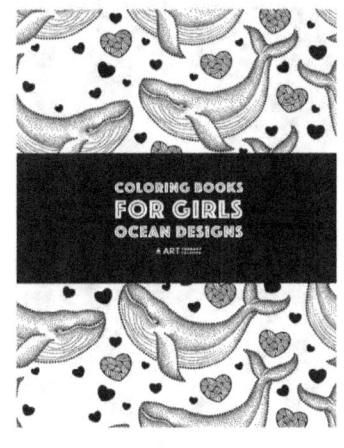

COLORING BOOKS FOR GIRLS OCEAN DESIGNS

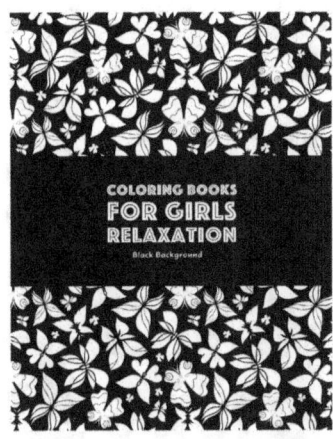

COLORING BOOKS FOR GIRLS RELAXATION
Black Background

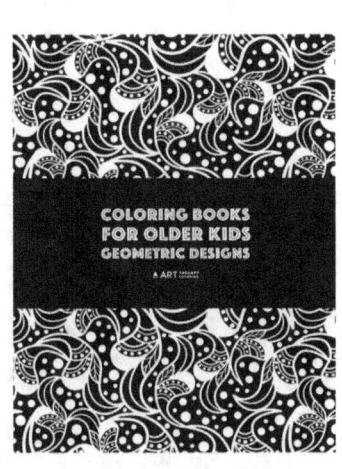

COLORING BOOKS FOR OLDER KIDS GEOMETRIC DESIGNS

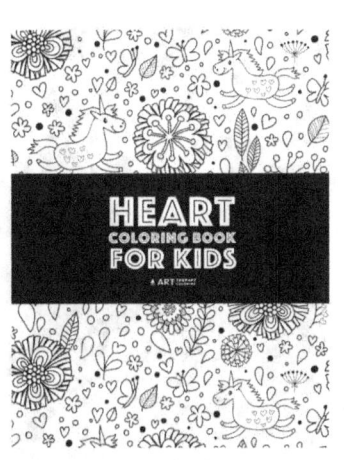

HEART COLORING BOOK FOR KIDS

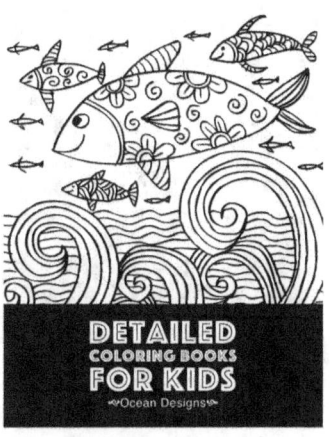

DETAILED COLORING BOOKS FOR KIDS
Ocean Designs

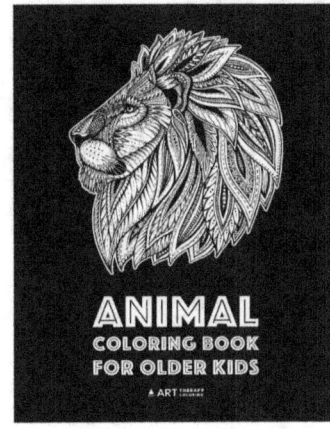

ANIMAL COLORING BOOK FOR OLDER KIDS

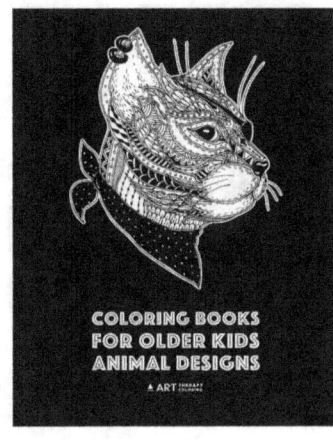

COLORING BOOKS FOR OLDER KIDS ANIMAL DESIGNS

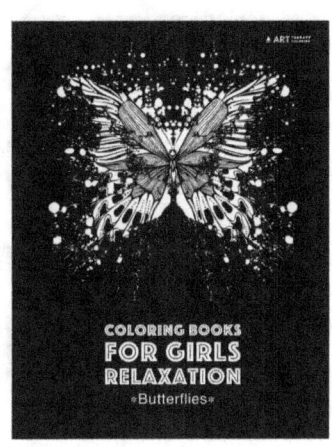

COLORING BOOKS FOR GIRLS RELAXATION
Butterflies

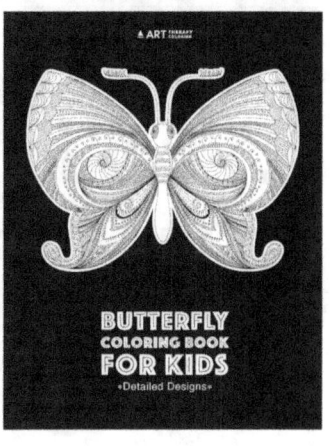

BUTTERFLY COLORING BOOK FOR KIDS
Detailed Designs

Coloring Books For Kids

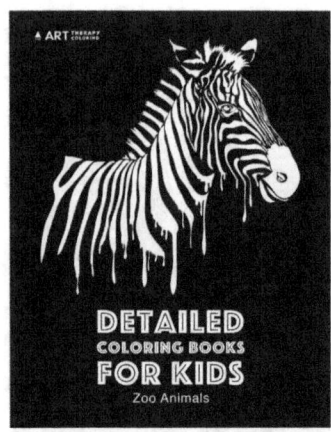

DETAILED
COLORING BOOKS
FOR KIDS
Zoo Animals

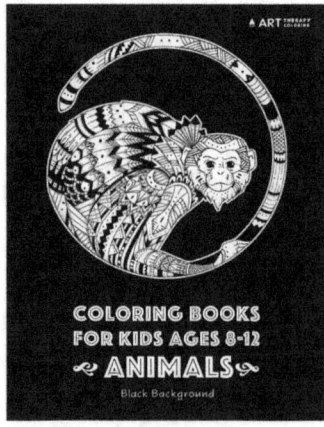

COLORING BOOKS
FOR KIDS AGES 8-12
ANIMALS
Black Background

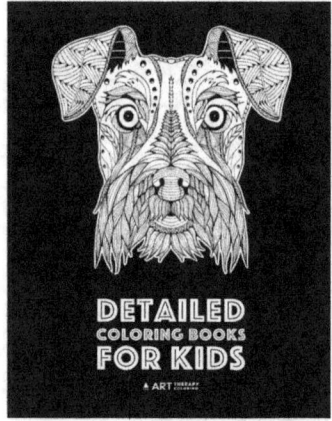

DETAILED
COLORING BOOKS
FOR KIDS

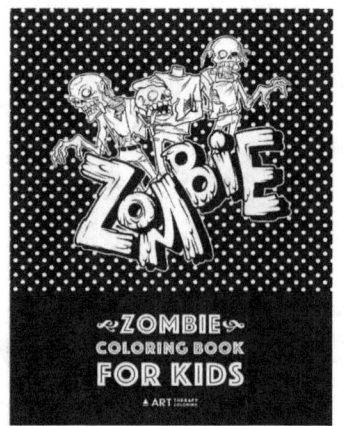

ZOMBIE
COLORING BOOK
FOR KIDS

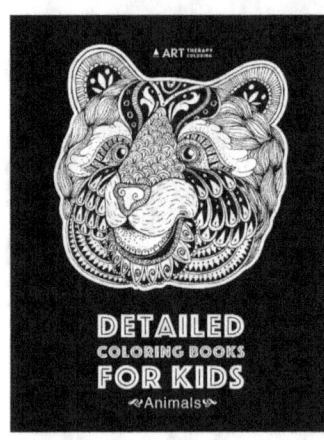

DETAILED
COLORING BOOKS
FOR KIDS
Animals

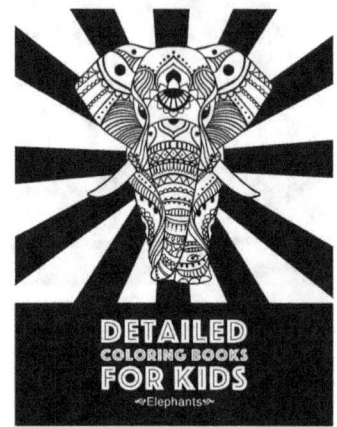

DETAILED
COLORING BOOKS
FOR KIDS
Elephants

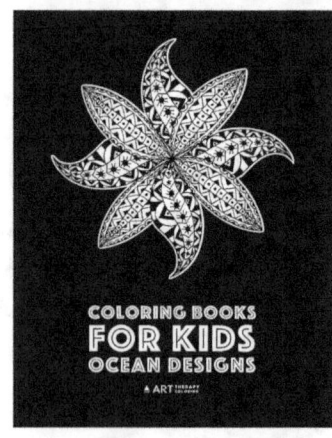

COLORING BOOKS
FOR KIDS
OCEAN DESIGNS

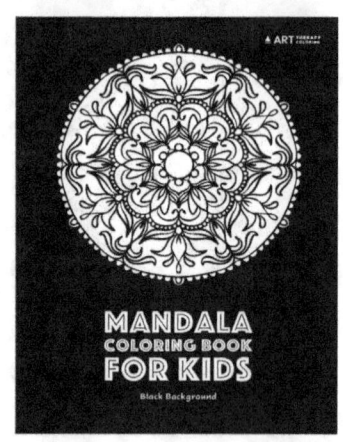

MANDALA
COLORING BOOK
FOR KIDS
Black Background

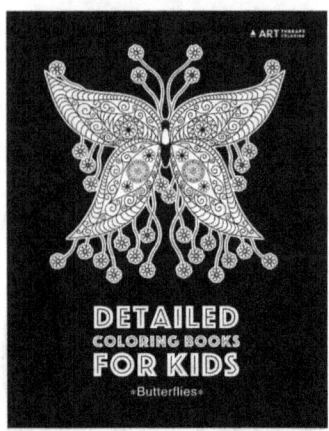

DETAILED
COLORING BOOKS
FOR KIDS
Butterflies

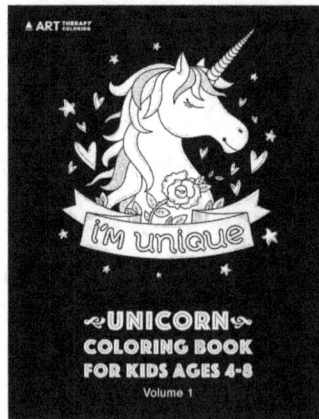

UNICORN
COLORING BOOK
FOR KIDS AGES 4-8
Volume 1

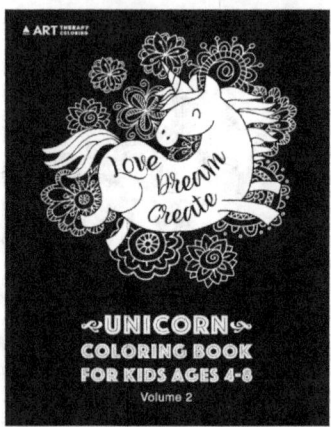

UNICORN
COLORING BOOK
FOR KIDS AGES 4-8
Volume 2

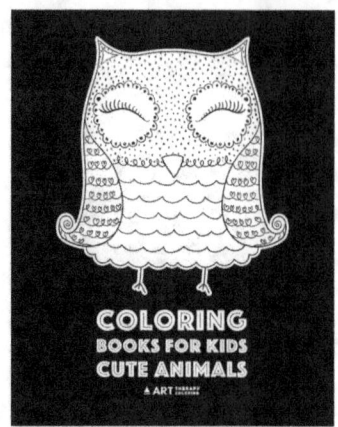

COLORING
BOOKS FOR KIDS
CUTE ANIMALS

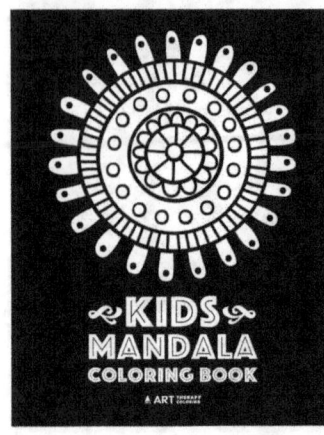

**KIDS
MANDALA**
COLORING BOOK

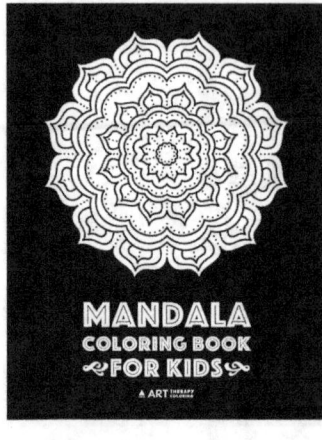

MANDALA
COLORING BOOK
FOR KIDS

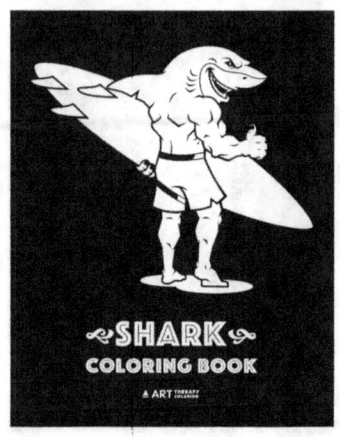

SHARK
COLORING BOOK

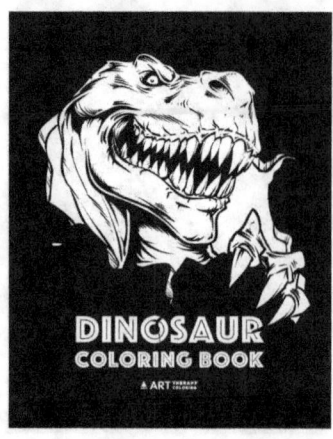

DINOSAUR
COLORING BOOK

Coloring Books For Adults

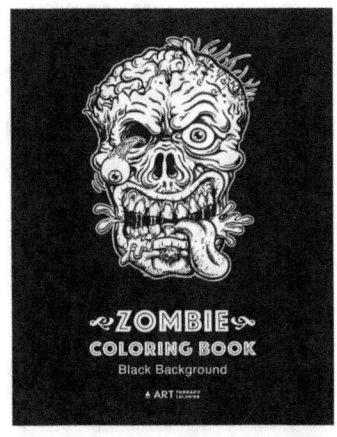

ZOMBIE
COLORING BOOK
Black Background

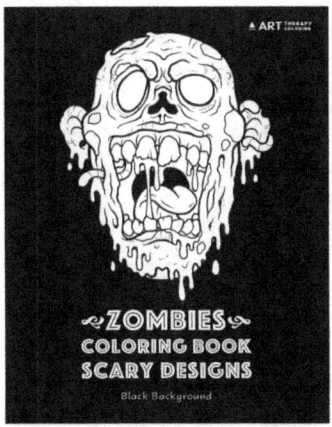

ZOMBIES
COLORING BOOK
SCARY DESIGNS
Black Background

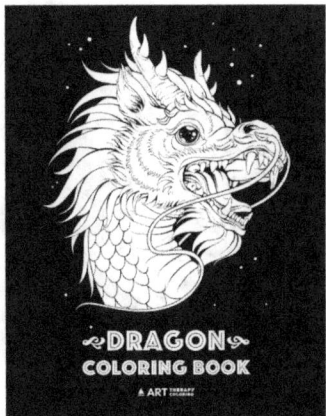

DRAGON
COLORING BOOK

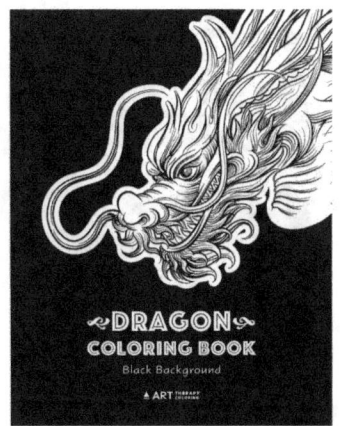

DRAGON
COLORING BOOK
Black Background

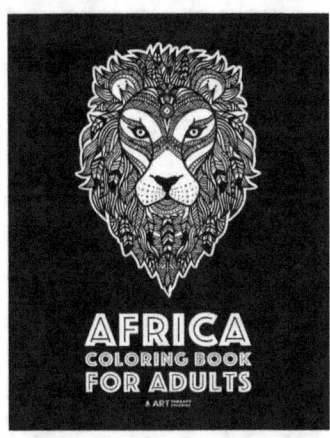

AFRICA
COLORING BOOK
FOR ADULTS

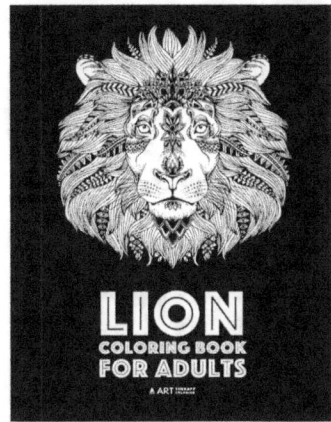

LION
COLORING BOOK
FOR ADULTS

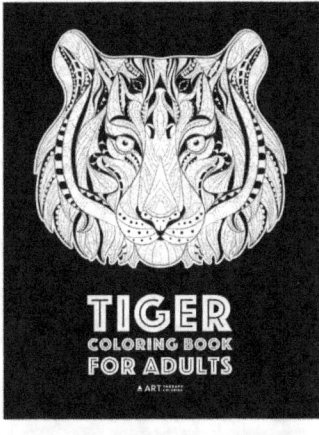

TIGER
COLORING BOOK
FOR ADULTS

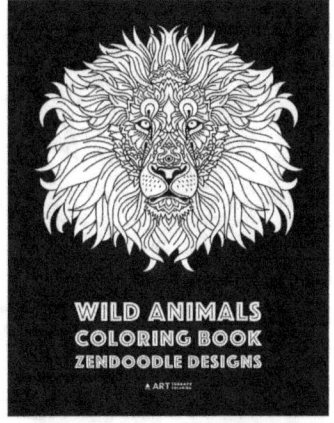

WILD ANIMALS
COLORING BOOK
ZENDOODLE DESIGNS

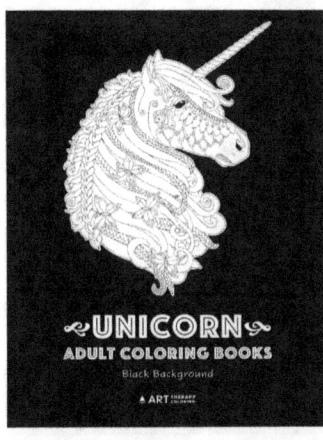

UNICORN
ADULT COLORING BOOKS
Black Background

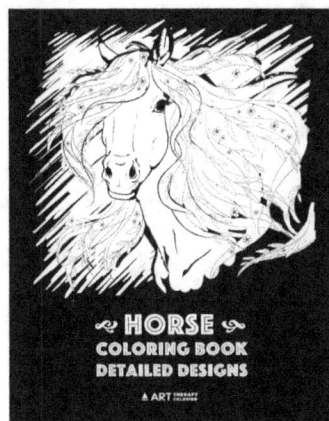

HORSE
COLORING BOOK
DETAILED DESIGNS

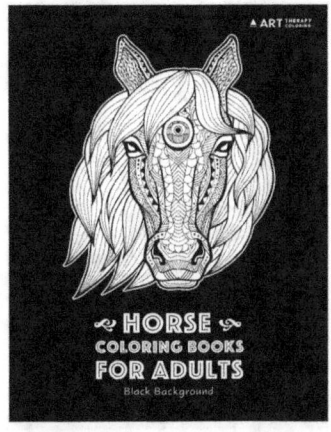

HORSE
COLORING BOOKS
FOR ADULTS
Black Background

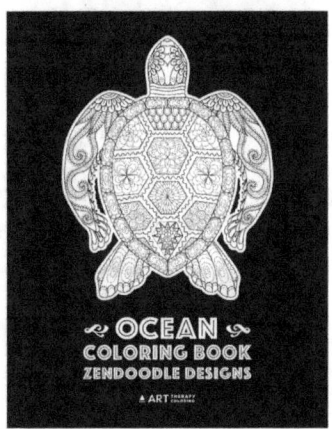

OCEAN
COLORING BOOK
ZENDOODLE DESIGNS

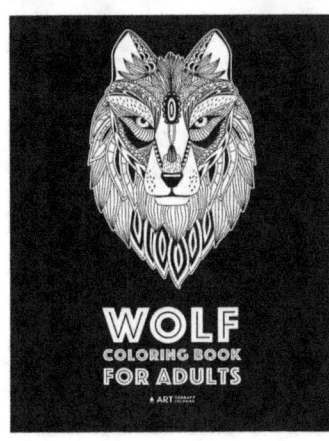

WOLF
COLORING BOOK
FOR ADULTS

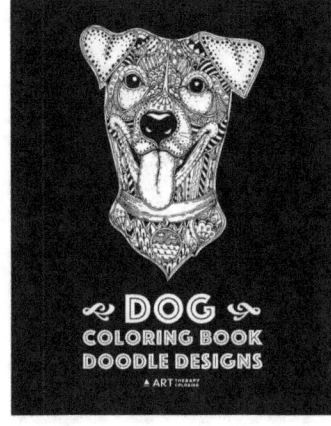

DOG
COLORING BOOK
DOODLE DESIGNS

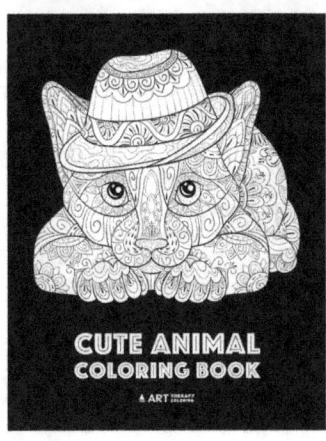

CUTE ANIMAL
COLORING BOOK

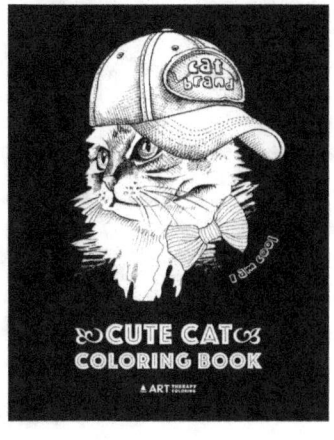

CUTE CAT
COLORING BOOK

Coloring Books For Adults

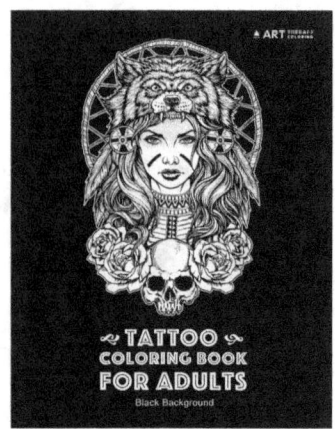

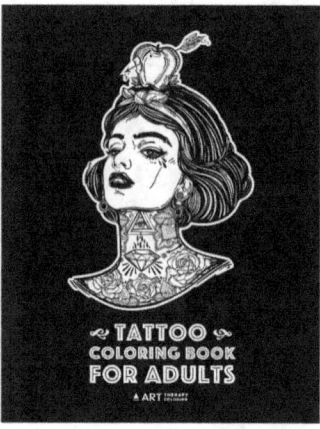

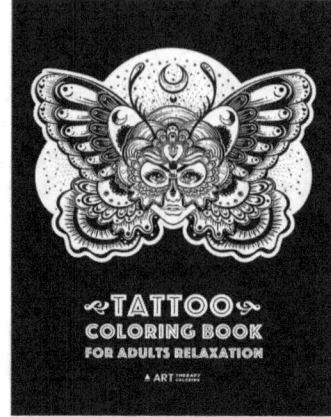

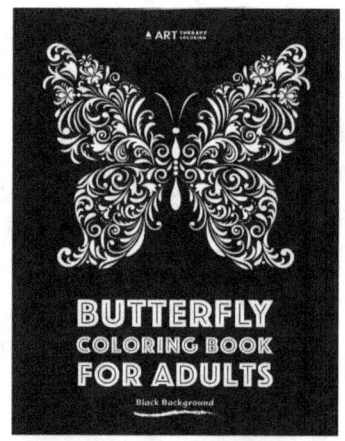

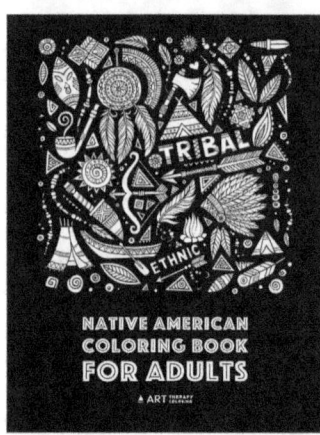

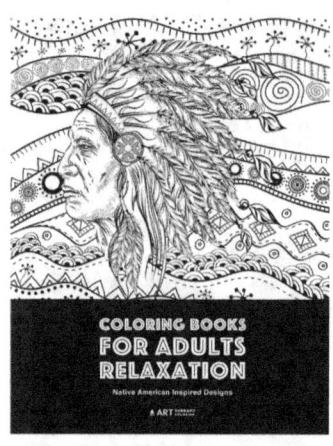

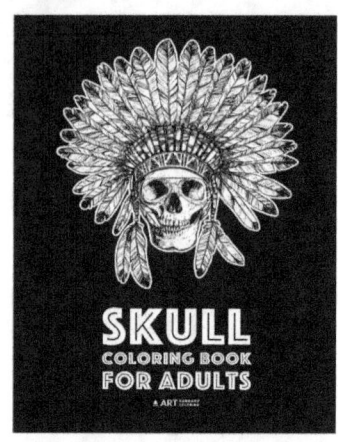

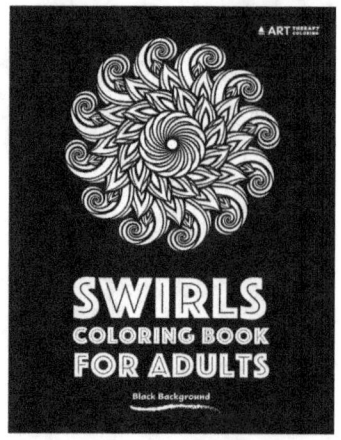

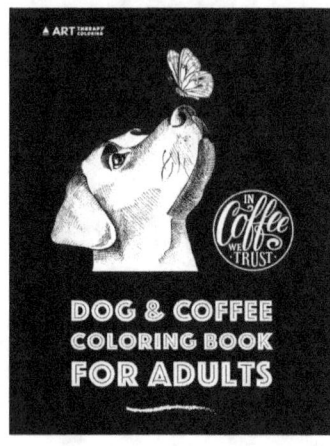

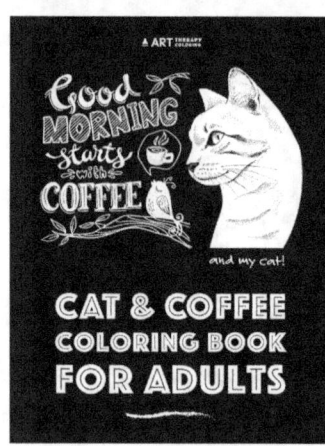

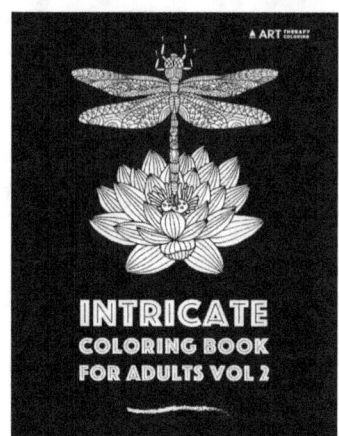

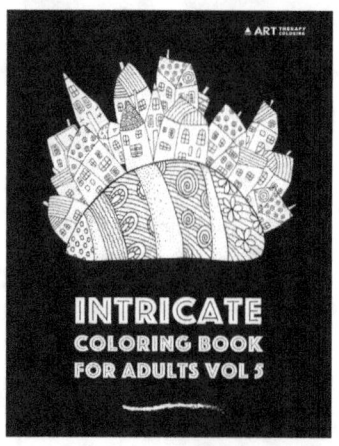

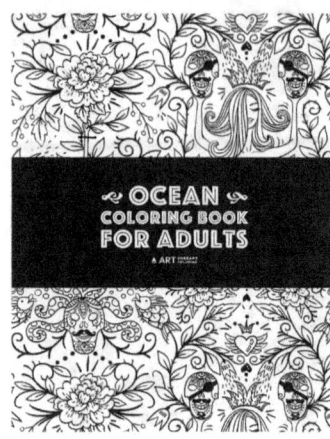

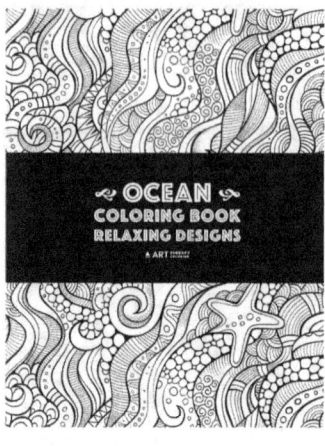

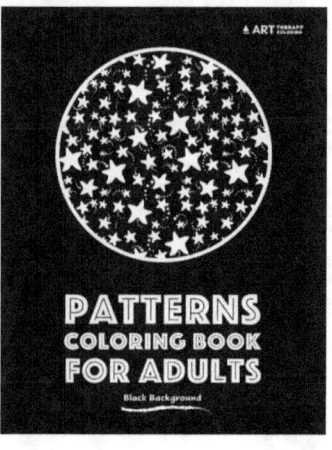

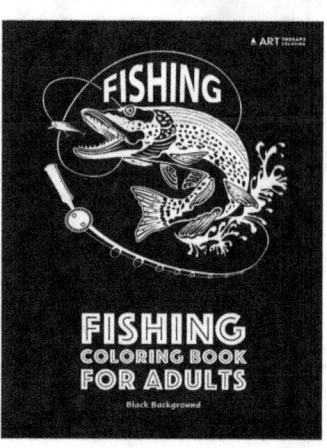

Coloring Books For Adults

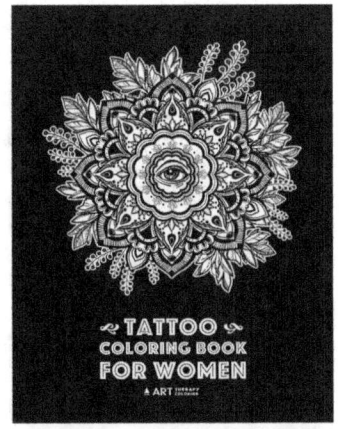

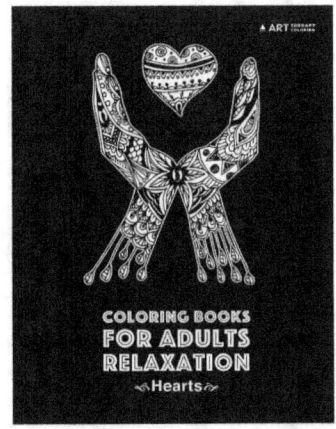

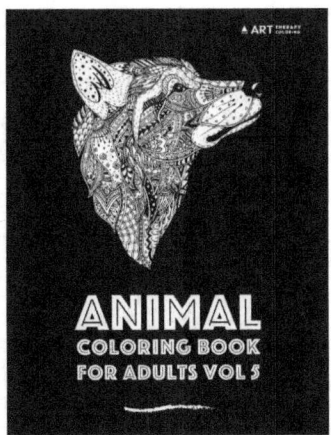

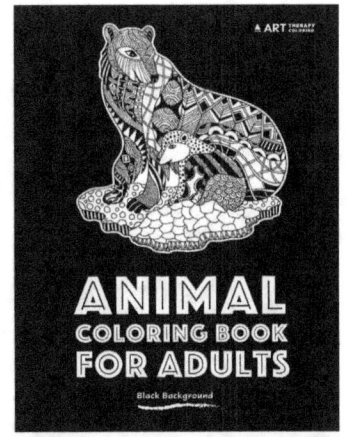

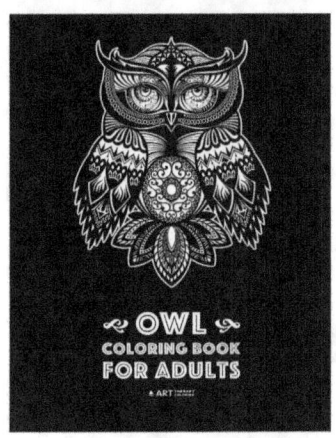

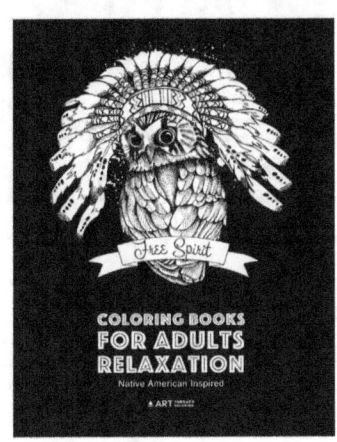

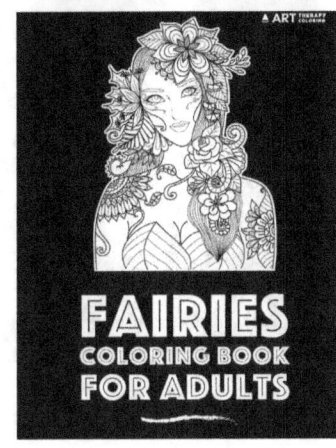

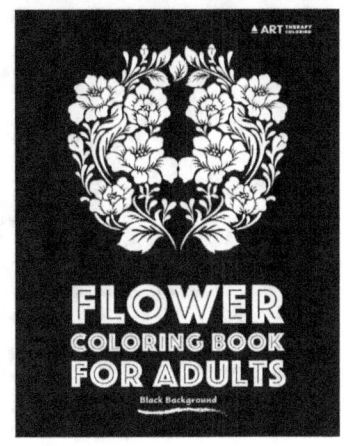

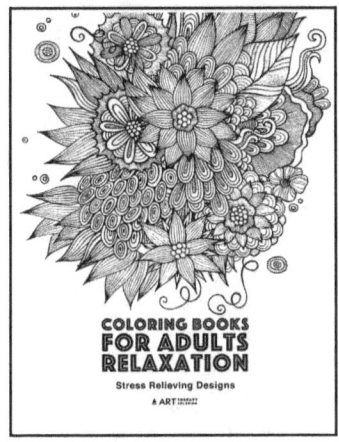

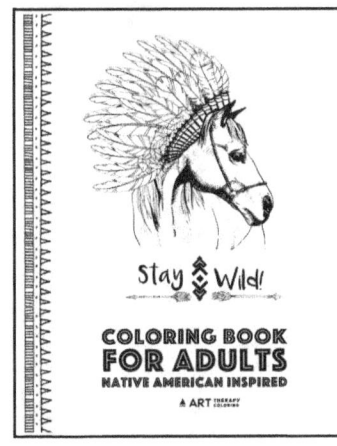

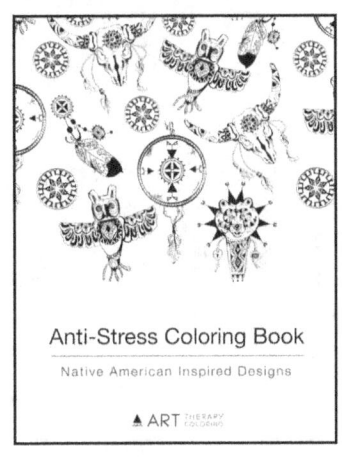

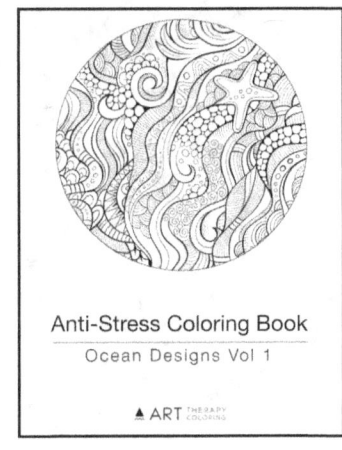

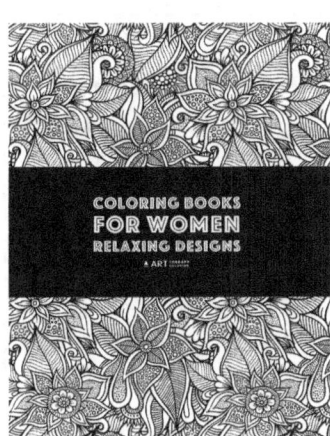

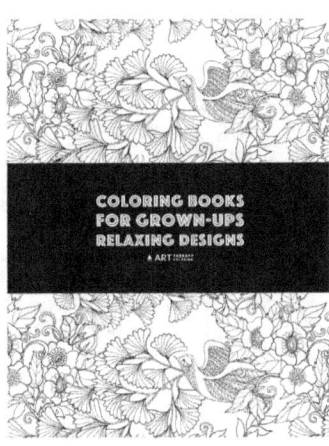

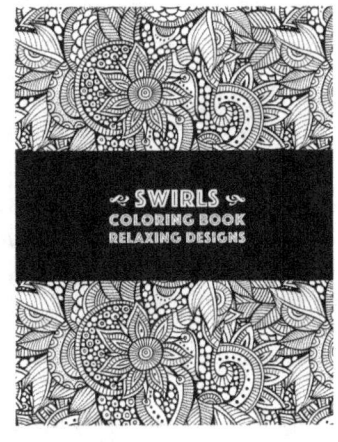

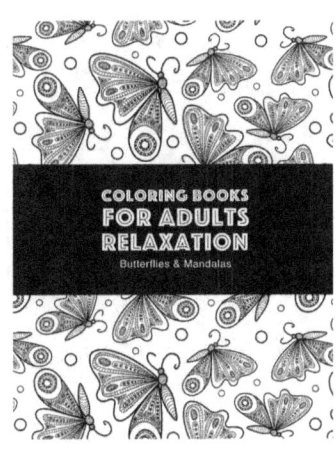

Coloring Books For Seniors

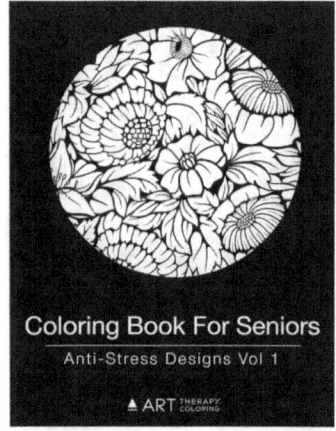

Coloring Book For Seniors
Anti-Stress Designs Vol 1

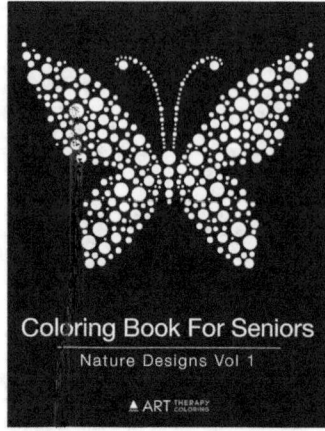

Coloring Book For Seniors
Nature Designs Vol 1

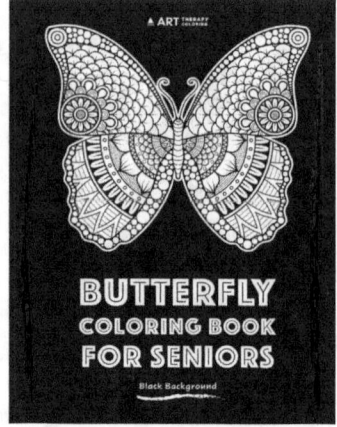

BUTTERFLY
COLORING BOOK
FOR SENIORS
Black Background

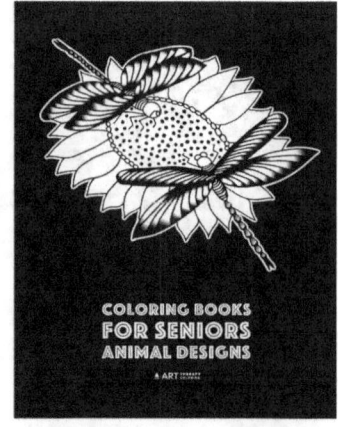

COLORING BOOKS
FOR SENIORS
ANIMAL DESIGNS

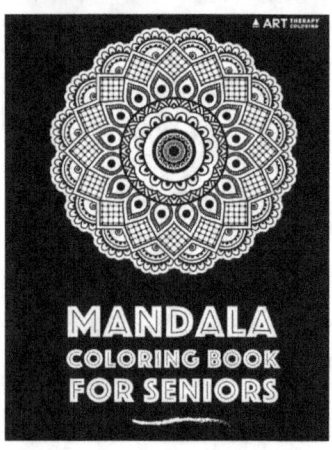

MANDALA
COLORING BOOK
FOR SENIORS

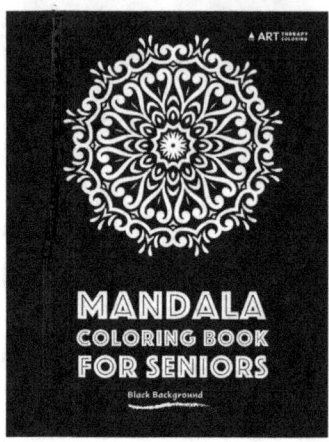

MANDALA
COLORING BOOK
FOR SENIORS
Black Background

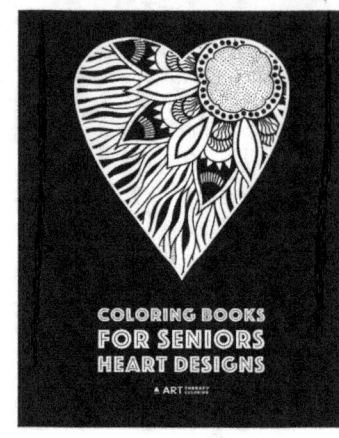

COLORING BOOKS
FOR SENIORS
HEART DESIGNS

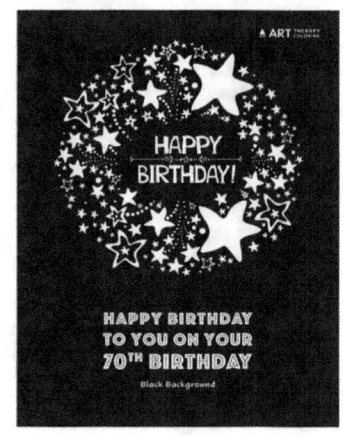

HAPPY BIRTHDAY
TO YOU ON YOUR
70TH BIRTHDAY
Black Background

COLORING BOOKS
FOR SENIORS
SWIRL DESIGNS
Black Background

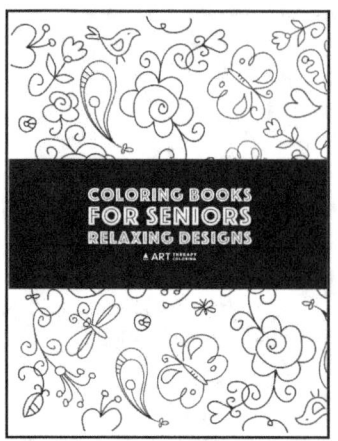

COLORING BOOKS
FOR SENIORS
RELAXING DESIGNS

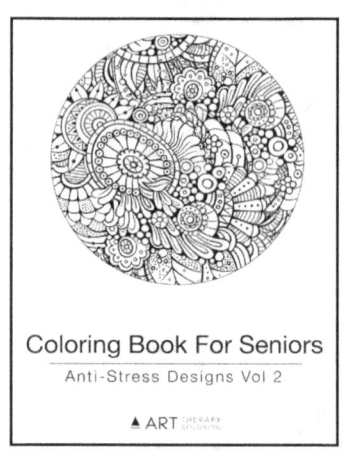

Coloring Book For Seniors
Anti-Stress Designs Vol 2

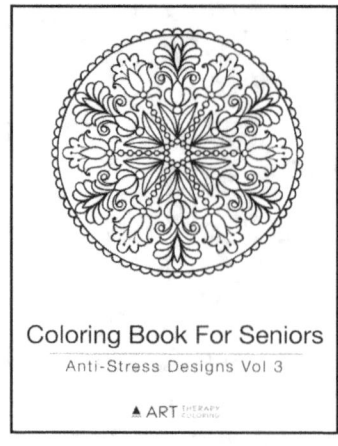

Coloring Book For Seniors
Anti-Stress Designs Vol 3

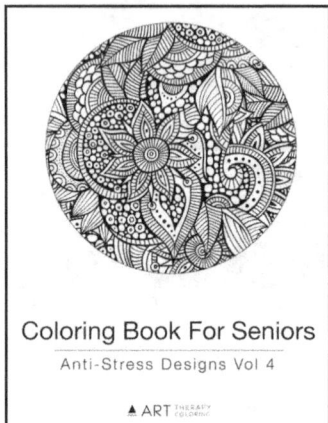

Coloring Book For Seniors
Anti-Stress Designs Vol 4

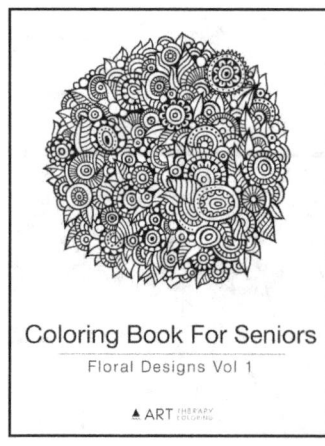

Coloring Book For Seniors
Floral Designs Vol 1

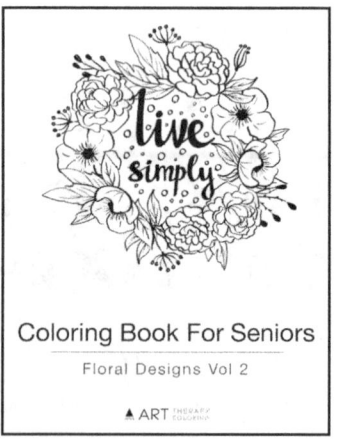

Coloring Book For Seniors
Floral Designs Vol 2

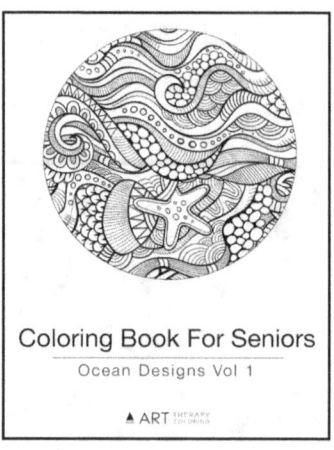

Coloring Book For Seniors
Ocean Designs Vol 1

Coloring Books For Men

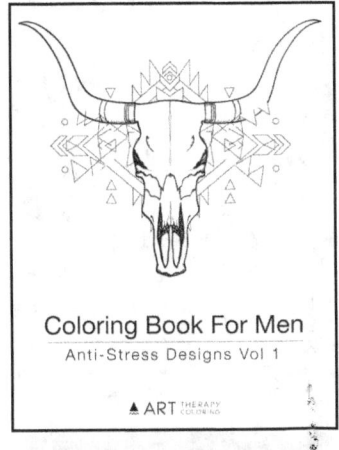

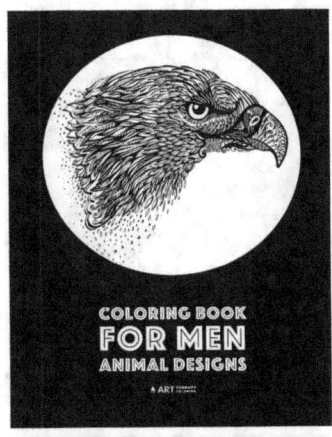

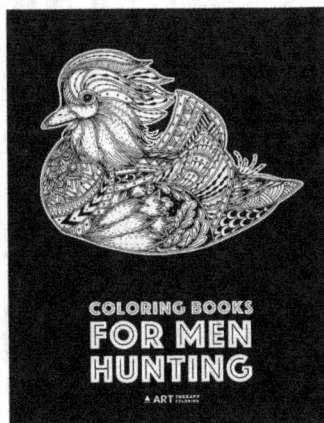

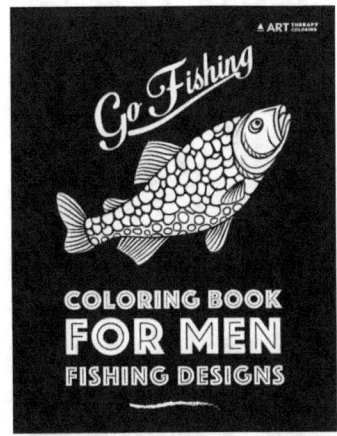

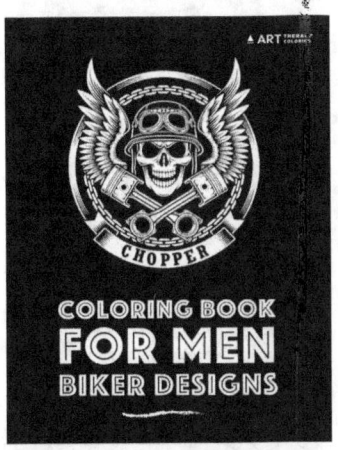

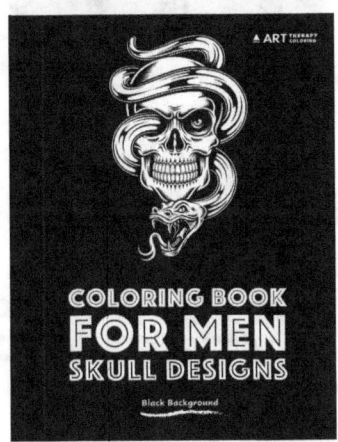

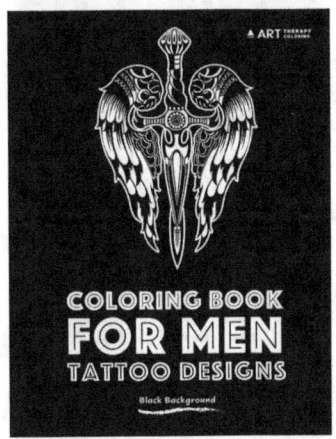

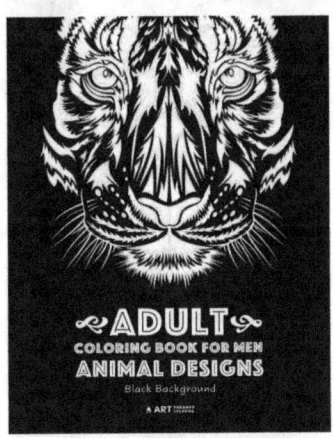

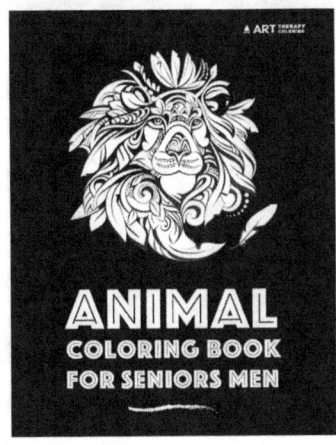

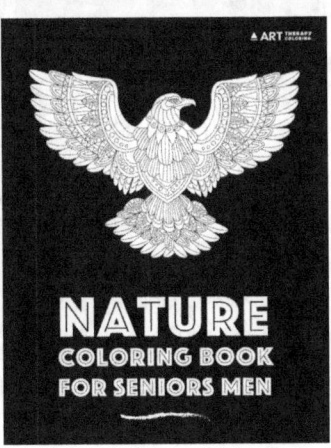

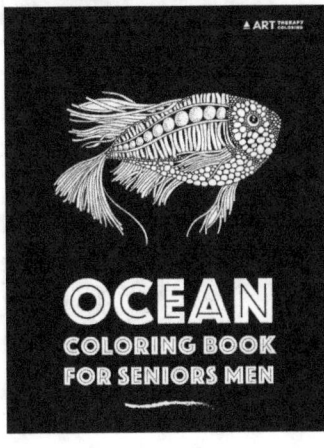

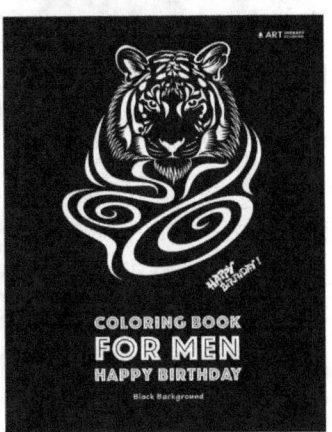

Coloring Books For Special Occasions

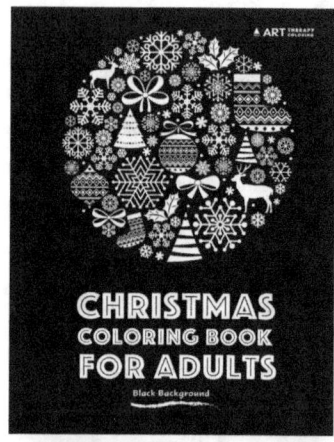 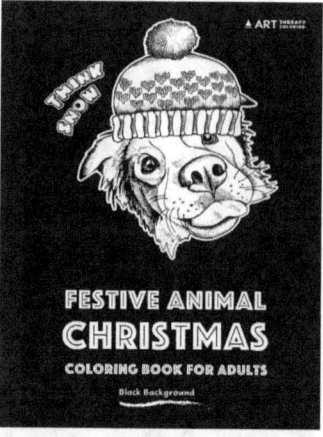 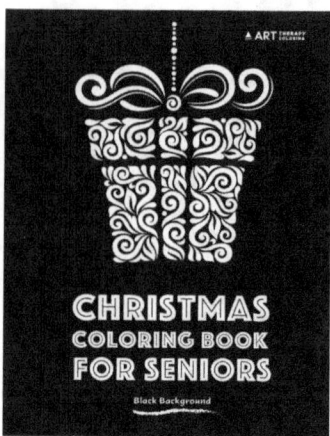 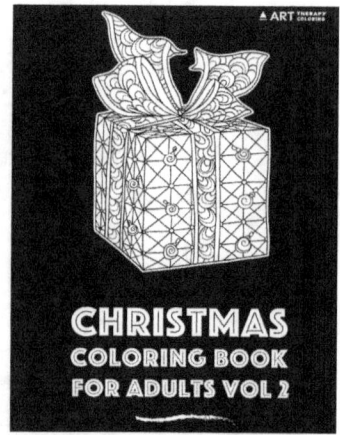

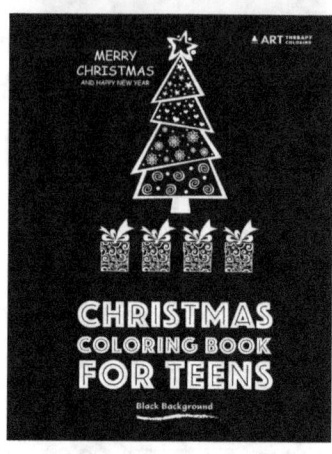 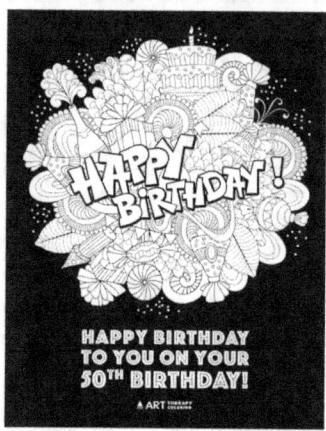 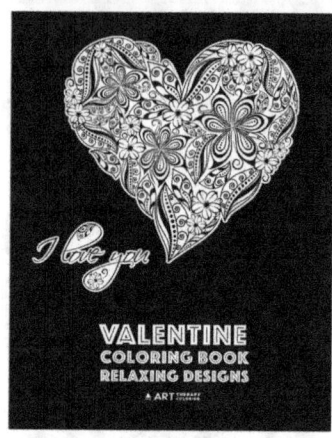 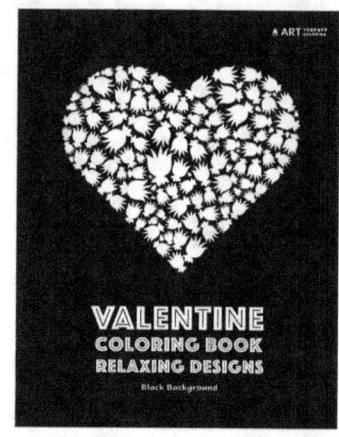

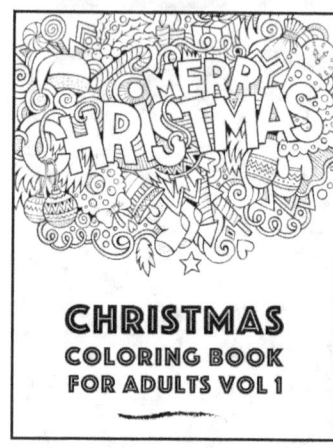 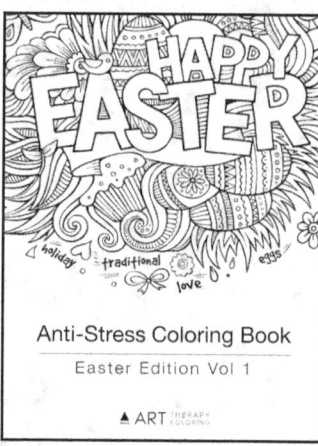 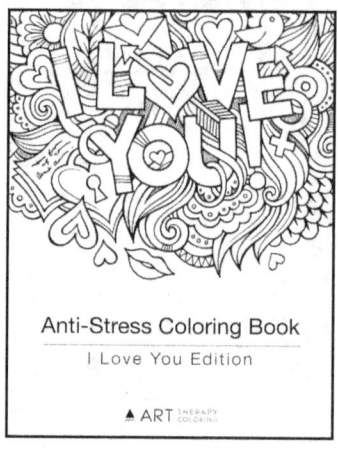 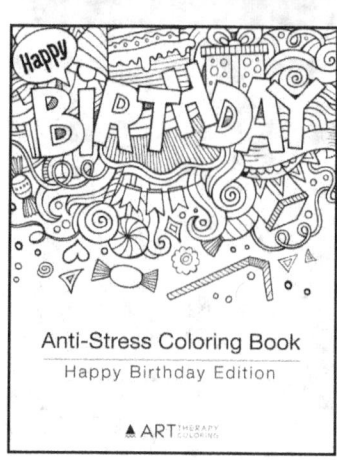

Motorcycle Coloring Book
For Teens: Black Background

Published by:
Art Therapy Coloring
El Dorado Hills, California
www.arttherapycoloring.com

ISBN: 978-1-944427-93-1